The Super Woman this journal belongs to is:

_____

If found, there's no reward—this is priceless to me.
But I know you're a super person,
so please return it by contacting me at:

_____

THE SUPER WOMAN JOURNAL

THE SUPER WOMAN JOURNAL

**Your Daily Guide to Becoming
Your Most Balanced,
Productive, Successful Self**

NICOLE LAPIN

BenBella Books, Inc.
10440 N. Central Expressway, Suite 800
Dallas, TX 75231
www.benbellabooks.com
Send feedback to feedback@benbellabooks.com

Printed in Malaysia
10 9 8 7 6 5 4 3 2 1

ISBN 9781948836364

Text design and composition by Aaron Edmiston
Cover design by Sophia Chang
Printed by TWP America, Inc.

Distributed to the trade by Two Rivers Distribution, an Ingram brand
www.tworiversdistribution.com

*To the Super Women who are committed to
getting it together and getting it all*

CONTENTS

Change only happens
when the discomfort of the
familiar outweighs the
fear of the unknown.

WHY I CREATED THIS JOURNAL

'm maybe the least likely person to be preaching balance. Years of *im*balance led me to a severe case of burnout and a subsequent breakdown. I'm talking actual rock-bottom.

It was only then that I realized I needed to rethink . . . everything.

I used to think:

- I would be balanced once I was successful.
- I would find balance with the right conditions. I often thought "I'll be balanced when . . ." or "I'd be balanced if only . . ."
- I needed to "make time" for "work/life" balance.

My former self meant well: she just didn't know better. I have compassion for that bitch but also a strong will never to go back to her habits. After my breakdown, I taught myself how to leave imbalance behind.

Here's what I know now:

- I had the equation wrong. I found myself more successful once I was balanced.
- There will always be "whens" and "if onlys" and surprises life throws at us. That imaginary finish line in your head? It doesn't exist.
- No one in the history of the world has figured out how to "make time." Balance is about making better choices now, with the time you have today. Oh, and that "work/life" stuff is bullshit. Work, family, your secret passion project . . . they are all part of one life—the only one you have.

But I also know that knowing better is not enough. I have to actively *do* better. We all know people who "know better" or "want to do better" and stay stuck in bad habits, never to actually get to "better." That's because "better" takes work. It takes lots and lots of reps at the gym to make muscles and it takes lots and lots of reps of healthy habits to make them stick.

Of course, shit happens. Life happens. Chaos, change, pain, loss, and all sorts of curveballs will come your way. You're not alone in this. The only thing certain in life is uncertainty. And when shit happens, you can only control how you respond. Will you be tempted to put this journal down and forget this "balance stuff" until better, calmer times come back around? Sure. Should you? *Hell no.* During the most chaotic seasons of your life you should be that much more diligent about taking the time to keep yourself on track.

There is no secret to achieving the balanced, successful life you want. Balance and productivity are skills. And as with any other skills, you have to practice them to get better—and stick with it when it gets hard. I will happily be your super woman trainer and cheerleader both in *Becoming Super Woman* and here in this journal, but I can't do this for you.

Maybe, even though I am not the most likely person to be preaching balance, I am exactly the person who should be, because I know what it's like both to lack it and to work hard to create and maintain it.

My former self on the verge of burnout needed this journal but didn't know it. That's why I created it for you. I hope it gives you the framework you need to practice living a balanced and productive life, day after day—no superpowers required.

Superwoman is the adversary of the women's movement.

—Gloria Steinem, ultimate women's rights advocate

WHY YOU NEED THIS JOURNAL

Time is your most valuable asset. You can always make more money, but you can't make more time (as hard as you might try). But it's not your only asset. Your attention and focus are right up there with it. Balance is not only about managing your time; it's also about managing your attention and focus.

And to do that, we first need to pay attention to what we are paying attention to. A lot of us are on autopilot, not even aware of where we are spending our time and placing our focus until we find ourselves somewhere we don't want to be.

While you may think you've got a handle on your general goals and values, have you actually spelled them out? Most of us have not. But, when you're going to a party, don't you want the exact address and all the details? Most of us do. After all, if you don't know exactly where you are going, how the fuck are you going to get there? (The party *and* your goal.)

What are your goals? Your values? Are you living in accordance with them and spending your time accordingly? If the answer to that last question is "Yes," awesome! Keep on keeping on, and use this journal to stay on track. But, if the answer is "No," or "I don't know," let's ask some bigger questions first.

You may have big goals and big dreams, but it's gonna be really hard to chase them down unless you get specific about what they are and organize your days around achieving them—and find a way to keep your balance in the process. Every single day life tugs us in a zillion different directions, trying to dictate what we do and tell us what's important. It's your job to resist the tug and decide what's important to *you*. So before you jump ahead to the daily pages, take some time with the next section to identify your goals and get real about your priorities.

YOUR GOALS

*S*o tell me what you want, what you really, really want. (I couldn't help myself.) In order to hold yourself accountable day in and day out, clear metrics are important. I love me some F-words, and in my first book, *Rich Bitch*, I preached three Fs of goal setting and planning: Finance, Family, and Fun. If you've read *Becoming Super Woman*, you know that after my breakdown, I realized my three Fs just weren't cutting it, and I added a fourth: Fitness. Fitness means mental and emotional fitness—self-care and therapy—in addition to physical health.

Within those categories, I set one-, three-, five-, seven-, and ten-year goals. Basically, I think about where I want to go in my life and reverse engineer my way there. This journal helps you do that on a daily scale, but the big picture comes first, so let's get F-ed up and set some goals. In the spirit of "I'll show you mine if you show me yours," here are my current Finance goals as an example to get you started:

My Finance Goals

Year 1: *Create a meaningful conversation and business verticals around Becoming Super Woman.*

Year 3: *Launch a platform of e-courses.*

Year 5: *Develop and host my own branded career summit.*

Year 7: *Pilot my own show about lifestyle and career issues, targeted at women.*

Year 10: *Launch my own platform featuring lifestyle and career content written by, produced by, and starring women.*

And, look at that, I've already nailed my Year 1 goal (hello, reader!) and am wwell underway on achieving my goal for Year 3. Having a clear outline for where I want my career to go has helped me to remain laser focused on getting there. I'm lucky to have new opportunities come my way a lot, but I say no to them more often than I say yes. Of course, if something super awesome comes along, it might be worth adjusting my goals, but in general, if an opportunity—even a great one—isn't helping me get where I want to go, then it's a distraction and I pass. Remember, if you try to do it all, you won't be doing much of it well.

Now, it's your turn:

My Finance Goals

Year 1: _____

_____

Year 3: _____

_____

Year 5: _____

_____

Year 7: _____

_____

Year 10: _____

_____

I won't bog this intro down with all my goals (if you really want those, you can find them in _Becoming Super Woman_) because this is not about me, it's about _you_, where _you_ are going and how _you_ are going to get there. Reaching your goals isn't about taking big leaps, it's about taking a bunch of little steps every day. So go ahead and think about what you want from the other areas of your life so you can take your daily steps with intention.

My Family Goals

Year 1: _____

_____

Year 3: _____

_____

Year 5: _____

_____

Year 7: _____

_____

Year 10: _____

_____

My Fun Goals

Year 1: _____

_____

Year 3: _____

_____

Year 5: _____

_____

Year 7: _____

_____

Year 10: _____

_____

My Fitness Goals

Year 1: _____

_____

Year 3: _____

_____

Year 5: _____

_____

Year 7: _____

_____

Year 10: _____

_____

Now that you've identified your goals, keep them at the top of your mind when scheduling your day. Each page, obviously, starts blank. It's up to you to determine how, specifically, it gets filled up. Naturally, there's a lot that *could* fit in a day, but the best fits are the actions that move you toward accomplishing your goals.

Of course, there are days when nothing you do moves you closer to your goals, and that's okay. Being balanced means being compassionate with yourself. But it also means being ultra self-aware. Don't beat yourself up when things don't go as planned; just notice and acknowledge it, and course correct with the aim of having more days on track than off.

YOUR PRIORITIES

The best way to ensure you stay on course more than you veer off is to navigate by your values and priorities. We're going to balance a budget of sorts—a budget of your time and energy. There are thousands of values you can choose from and thousands of ways to prioritize them, but for now, let's start with five of the most common areas of our lives that we value and try (and often struggle) to juggle:

1. Career
2. Romance
3. Family & Friends
4. Physical Health
5. Emotional Wellness

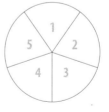

All these areas of your life are not going to get or need equal attention at every moment. In fact, the size of the various pieces of this pie chart will not only vary for everyone, they will change over time. Having your areas of focus broken down will help you reflect on exactly what you value and how much you value it. Don't shame yourself for not focusing on things you've actively decided you're not going to focus on at a certain time. If you are building a new career and letting romance take a back seat or taking time out for family and letting work wait, that's fine, as long as you are doing it intentionally. By definition, you can't prioritize everything—that's not how priorities work. It might be how we imagine Superwoman operating—trying to do it all, all the time—but it's not how we super women work and thrive.

So let's decide what values you want to focus on and how you want to prioritize them. You get ten points. You have your five categories. Now, we're going to divvy up those ten points among the five categories.

Here's an example of how I first completed this exercise, years ago:

1. Career: 7
2. Romance: 1
3. Family & Friends: 1
4. Physical Health: 1
5. Emotional Wellness: 0

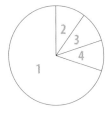

Total: 10 points

You'll notice I allocated *zero* points to Emotional Wellness . . . and we all know where that got me. So, my point allocation looks a bit different these days, with three whole points allocated to that particular category. You get the idea. We live, we learn, we adjust. We eat pie.

How many points do you want to allot to each of your priorities? What is truly important to you? What do you need to focus on to reach your goals?

1. Career: _____
2. Romance: _____
3. Family & Friends: _____
4. Physical Health: _____
5. Emotional Wellness: _____

Total: 10 points

Change the categories if you want; for the pie charts on the daily pages, I've even given you an extra in case you decide you want a sixth category. The categories I outlined above fit nicely into our 4 Fs: Finance (career), Family (family & friends, romance) Fun (all of the above), and Fitness (Emotional Wellness and physical health). That's intentional; your goals should align with your priorities so that both are reflected in the choices you make about how to spend your day.

Four categories or six—all I ask is that you:
- give at least one point to Emotional Wellness (because if you don't, it will catch up with you and demand all of them)
- be honest with yourself.

You can value being wealthy and prioritize making money. That's cool; just own that that's what you're doing. These categories aren't about what you think you *should* value. If you are trying to adopt values that aren't truly yours, you'll never act in accordance with them. No one sees this but you, and no one lives your life but you.

Your day, your life, your rules. The best thing about making the rules is that you have a 100 percent chance of winning. Use this journal as your playbook for a life that's balanced—whatever balanced looks like for you.

A common analogy for balance is walking a tight-rope, and it's a good one: in order to make it across you have to focus *both* on the goal and the steps you're taking right now. One or the other doesn't work. If you aren't mindful of your footing in the present, you'll fall. If you're looking down at your feet instead of focusing on where you're headed, you'll fall.

This journal helps you fly, not fall, and ultimately have it all. And hell yes, women can have it all . . . but only by defining for themselves what having it all looks like (I'm guessing it's not nonstop stress and trying to "do it all"). Your goals, your values, your priorities: that's what "having it all" is to you, Super Woman. Now, it's time to get it together and *get* it all.

Simple Math:
Super Woman > Superwoman

PRO TIPS ON PRODUCTIVITY

Starting the day with a plan is a good, well . . . start, but staying productive throughout the day in the face of distractions is a skill (even, I might venture, a superpower). I've interviewed hundreds—if not thousands—of very productive people and I can tell you that they are not magically productive; they have systems they have perfected over the years to work like magic for them. Everyone finds their own productivity hacks and ways to shore up lagging motivation, but here are a few of my field-tested *do*s and *don't*s.

- *Don't* cancel personal plans because you feel like you are "too busy" to work out or see a friend.
- *Do* prioritize the activities, events, or tasks that make you feel good and those that contribute most to your overall productivity (typically, those to-do items with a 24-hour time window and those that move you toward your goals).
- *Don't* schedule something for thirty minutes or an hour just because that looks organized

on your calendar. If a meeting should only take ten minutes, then great, the meeting can be over and you just got twenty minutes of your valuable time back. Determine whether holding a meeting in person is something you need to do, or whether it would it be more efficient to discuss on Skype—or better yet, via email. Be sure to factor in the added time for getting ready and traveling to and from each meeting.

- *Do* streamline your choices. It's no coincidence that Steve Jobs had a "uniform" of jeans and a black shirt. Simon Cowell and Mark Cuban have been known for this, too. Think that's only a guy thing? Nope. The uber super woman Jenna Lyons (who transformed J.Crew into the megabrand it is today) minimizes her wardrobe staples so that she can just reach into her closet and know she'll pull out a winner. Plan your meals; designate certain days or certain times of day for certain tasks; and lean on schedules, routines, and habits. Having to make fewer mundane choices throughout the day leaves more time (and brainpower) for making the important ones.

- *Don't* ignore your body clock and how you feel at various times of day. Take your natural rhythms into consideration when planning your schedule. Within the first two to four hours of waking up, your brain is the sharpest it's going to be all day, and research shows that the afternoon, specifically 3 PM, is the most optimal time for activities like meetings. Your body is on your side; trust that bitch.

- *Do* chill when your energy drops in the late afternoon (it happens to everyone . . . not because of eating a big lunch but due to a predictable circadian rhythm). Take some down time at your desk or with a colleague to quietly regroup for the rest of the day.

Finally, I want to quickly discuss the difference between some words that we have come to think of as meaning the same thing, but which are actually quite different.

- *"Busy" v. "Productive."* I get it, you're "sooooo busy." "Busy" is that never-ending laundry list of all the things you *indiscriminately think you should do*, regardless of their lack of urgency or value to your day. They are the tasks that have to get done at some point, but that leave you feeling scattered when you complete them as they arise: firing off email responses, picking up dry-cleaning, making appointments and phone calls. Being "productive" means doing the things you *consciously prioritize*: nailing a major deadline at work, attending your favorite workout class, and checking in with a close friend who is going through a tough time. Sure, it can also mean running errands or making calls, but the productive way to attend to those tasks is to set aside time to do them— when they truly need to be done.

- *"Urgent" v. "Important."* Because of our connectivity we tend to view all emails and texts that come in as "urgent." But, just because two emails come in at the same time doesn't mean they are of equal weight or priority. "Urgent" messages are things that legitimately have a deadline or short horizon of opportunity. "Important" messages are ones that carry weight but can, well, wait. At the same time, many of the tasks that move you toward your goals are important, but not necessarily urgent. If you find you are never getting from the urgent to the important, you may need to make some changes.

There is much more about this in *Becoming Super Woman*—a whole chapter, in fact—but to sum up, your job each day is to figure out how to be productive and not just busy by prioritizing things that are truly urgent while discerning and thoughtfully procrastinating on what may be important but doesn't need immediate attention. The differences are subtle but the words you use matter when mapping out what matters in your day.

USING THE DAILY PAGES

Thinking about your big goals and dreams for the future can be overwhelming. Thinking about the endless responsibilities and demands of the present can be overwhelming, too. The best way to get over the overwhelm is to connect the dots between your future and your present, one day at a time. And the best way to live a life you love is to remind yourself what you love about the life you're living. That's what *The Super Woman Journal* helps you do.

PLAN

The left-hand page is a space for you to *plan*. Take a few minutes every morning and think about where you want to go and how you're going to get there.

Today's priorities:

What you put here can be as specific or as general as you want. It can be "Sales report" or "Look for moments of joy." It can be "Family" or "Finish presentation." You can set one priority or two; use this as a space to remind yourself of a big goal or to record the one thing that, if you completed it, would make the day a success. Two things to consider here are what most needs to be worked on or finished today and what is most important to you or what you most want to focus on. Look at the F lists you made to remind yourself what you're ultimately working toward: this month, this year, and for the future.

Tasks that will move me toward my goals:

Ask yourself the same two questions I mentioned above: what most needs to be worked on or finished today and what is most important to you. This isn't a laundry list of everything you *could* do today—these are the things that will have the biggest impact in the short term or that will move you furthest on the path to your goals. What do you have to do? What do you want to do? Which of the latter aligns with your values and priorities?

Once you have your task list, rank your tasks on the right in order of urgency and importance.

Today I will take care of myself by:

Make sure you're making yourself a priority. What will you do today to safeguard and build your Emotional Wellness?

REFLECT

The right-hand page is your opportunity to *reflect*. When your day is over, look back on how you spent it and appreciate the awesome life you already have.

Today I spent my time on:

Write in the names of the priority categories you identified earlier and shade in the number of pieces corre-
sponding to how much time and energy you devoted
to each. Remember, the daily allocation doesn't have
to line up with the point allocation you set on page 25.
Maybe your goal was to devote three points to Family overall, but that doesn't mean that you should have
three pieces of your Family pie shaded in every day.
Some days you might shade in the whole Career pie,
other days none of it. What matters is the trends you
notice over time. If you said on page 25 that your goal
was to allocate five points to Career and you are consis-
tently shading in that whole pie, that's a sign that you
either aren't living according to your priorities or that
you need to revisit what your priorities truly are. Either
way, a change is in order, Super Woman. This is your
space to cultivate awareness of how you are actually
spending your one and only life.

Today I am grateful for:

Gratitude is a proven way to give your Emotional Wellness a boost. It is easy to obsess over what went wrong
or what you wish you'd done differently, but ending the
day by focusing on what you have will help you love the
super life you're living right now.

Date: *October 8, 2019*

I never dreamed about success. I worked for it.

—Estée Lauder

Today's priorities:

Finish writing script for video

Remember to be mindful and present

Tasks that will move me toward my goals: Rank

☐ *Video script* | *1*

☐ *Make travel plans for next month* | *5*

☐ *Go over social media strategy* | *2*

☐ *Sign up for new class* | *3*

☐ *Start deck for presentation* | *4*

☐ |

☐ |

☐ |

☐ |

Today I will take care of myself by:

Meditating for 20 minutes (and writing in this journal!)

Today I spent my time on:

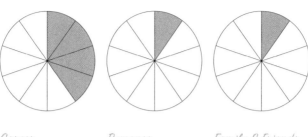

Career _____ Romance _____ Family & Friends _____

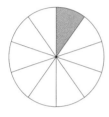

Physical Health _____ Emotional Wellness _____

Today I am grateful for:

Having the opportunity to do work I love with people I

respect. Also coffee. _____

_____

_____

_____

_____

_____

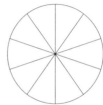

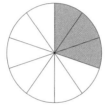

A QUICK NOTE
ABOUT HABIT

Healthy habits are tough to stick to. Studies have shown that it takes about two months (or sixty-six days) to create a lasting one. The best way to do that is to set up a habit "loop," which consists of three parts: 1) a cue, 2) the habit, and 3) a reward. Most healthy habits don't stick because we forget about the reward part. I mean, what would you actually do over and over again if you got nothing back ever? Nada.

Here's how I made my daily check ins . . . actually happen daily:

Morning Cue: I program my coffee maker at 7 AM. When I smell the aroma, I know it's time for *The Super Woman Journal*.

Habit: I spend five minutes crafting my most successful, productive, and balanced day by connecting the dots between my goals and my plans.

Reward: I drink that yummy coffee with cinnamon and almond milk.

Evening Cue: I put on my lotion before bed. When I smell the white musk (old school, I know), I know it's time for *The Super Woman Journal*.

Habit: I reflect on my day for five minutes to be mindful of the life I am living, noticing how I've spent my time and ending my day with gratitude.

Reward: I put the journal down and dive into one of the three books on my nightstand.

Your turn: How can you tie your journaling time into your day to make it a habit and make it happen?

Morning Cue: _____

_____

_____

Habit: _____

_____

_____

Reward: _____

_____

_____

Evening Cue: _____

_____

_____

Habit: _____

_____

_____

Reward: _____

_____

_____

*The world will see you
the way you see you,
and treat you the way
you treat yourself.*

—**Beyoncé**

YOUR COMMITMENT

I f you're picking up this journal, it means you're ready to become the most balanced, productive version of yourself: to become a Super Woman. Congrats! Committing to writing in this journal even a few days per week will do more to set you up for success than you can imagine.

If you worry that making this commitment to yourself is impossible with all the obligations you have, well . . . it's not. We *all* have demands pulling at us and creating a false sense of urgency. But they say "put your oxygen mask on first" for a reason. If you try to be all things to everyone else, you are in danger of becoming nothing to yourself.

Here's the commitment I made to myself:

I, *Nicole Lapin*, am not Superwoman, who takes care of everyone and everything before myself. I am a Super Woman who puts my needs first so I can be the most successful, productive, balanced version of me. Not being selfless is not selfish, it is self-care.

This journal is important to my self-care because *it reminds me that while I have a crew of other Super Women who have my back, I am the captain of my own destiny* .

It reminds me that *I am a masterpiece and also a work in progress*.

I am committed to *making it work with my first love (duh, it's me)*.

Now fill in the blanks with your commitment to yourself:
I, _____, am not Superwoman, who takes care of everyone and everything before myself. I am a Super Woman who puts my needs first so I can be the most successful, productive, balanced version of me. Not being selfless is not selfish, it is self-care.

This journal is important to my self-care because

_____

_____.

It reminds me that _____

_____.

I am committed to _____

_____.

THE JOURNAL

THE SUPER WOMAN JOURNAL ● PLAN

I never dreamed about success. I worked for it.

—Estée Lauder

Today's priorities:

_____

_____

Tasks that will move me toward my goals: *Rank*

☐ _____ | ____

☐ _____ | ____

☐ _____ | ____

☐ _____ | ____

☐ _____ | ____

☐ _____ | ____

☐ _____ | ____

☐ _____ | ____

☐ _____ | ____

Today I will take care of myself by:

_____

_____

Today I spent my time on:

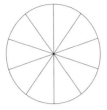 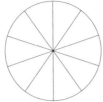 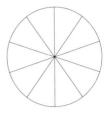

_____   _____   _____

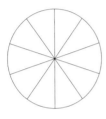 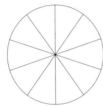 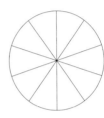

_____   _____   _____

Today I am grateful for:

_____

_____

_____

_____

_____

_____

_____

Date: _____

If you just set out to be liked, you would be prepared to compromise on anything at any time, and you would achieve nothing.

—Margaret Thatcher

Today's priorities:

_____

_____

Tasks that will move me toward my goals: *Rank*

☐ _____ | _____

☐ _____ | _____

☐ _____ | _____

☐ _____ | _____

☐ _____ | _____

☐ _____ | _____

☐ _____ | _____

☐ _____ | _____

☐ _____ | _____

Today I will take care of myself by:

_____

_____

Today I spent my time on:

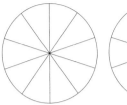 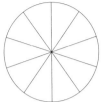 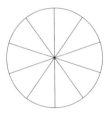

_____   _____   _____

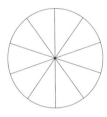 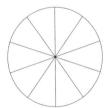 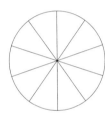

_____   _____   _____

Today I am grateful for:

_____

_____

_____

_____

_____

_____

_____

Date: _____

If we could give every individual the right amount of nourishment and exercise, not too little and not too much, we would have found the safest way to health.

—Hippocrates

Today's priorities:

_____

_____

Tasks that will move me toward my goals:　　　　　　　*Rank*

☐ _____ | ____

☐ _____ | ____

☐ _____ | ____

☐ _____ | ____

☐ _____ | ____

☐ _____ | ____

☐ _____ | ____

☐ _____ | ____

☐ _____ | ____

Today I will take care of myself by:

_____

_____

Today I spent my time on:

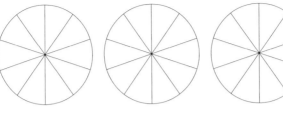

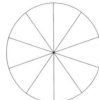

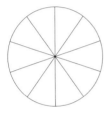

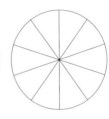

Today I am grateful for:

_____

_____

_____

_____

_____

_____

_____

Date: _____

The challenge is not to be perfect . . . it's to be whole.

—Jane Fonda

Today's priorities:

_____

_____

Tasks that will move me toward my goals: *Rank*

☐ _____ | ____

☐ _____ | ____

☐ _____ | ____

☐ _____ | ____

☐ _____ | ____

☐ _____ | ____

☐ _____ | ____

☐ _____ | ____

☐ _____ | ____

Today I will take care of myself by:

_____

_____

Today I spent my time on:

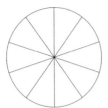 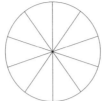 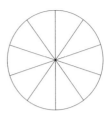

_____ _____ _____

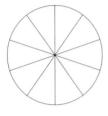 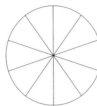 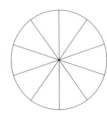

_____ _____ _____

Today I am grateful for:

_____

_____

_____

_____

_____

_____

_____

Date: _____

You are the one that possesses the keys to your being. You carry the passport to your own happiness.

—Diane von Furstenberg

Today's priorities:

_____

_____

Tasks that will move me toward my goals:　　　　　　　*Rank*

☐ _____ | ___

☐ _____ | ___

☐ _____ | ___

☐ _____ | ___

☐ _____ | ___

☐ _____ | ___

☐ _____ | ___

☐ _____ | ___

☐ _____ | ___

Today I will take care of myself by:

_____

_____

Today I spent my time on:

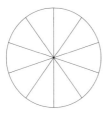 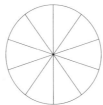 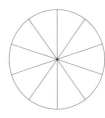

_____   _____   _____

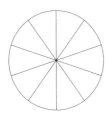 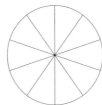 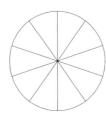

_____   _____   _____

Today I am grateful for:

_____

_____

_____

_____

_____

_____

_____

Date: _____

As a leader, it's a major responsibility on your shoulders to practice the behavior you want others to follow.

—Himanshu Bhatia

Today's priorities:

_____

_____

Tasks that will move me toward my goals: *Rank*

☐ _____ | ____

☐ _____ | ____

☐ _____ | ____

☐ _____ | ____

☐ _____ | ____

☐ _____ | ____

☐ _____ | ____

☐ _____ | ____

☐ _____ | ____

Today I will take care of myself by:

_____

_____

Today I spent my time on:

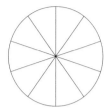 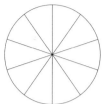 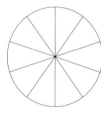

_____ _____ _____

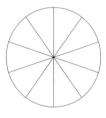 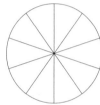 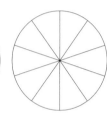

_____ _____ _____

Today I am grateful for:

_____

_____

_____

_____

_____

_____

_____

Date: _____

You have trust in what you think. If you splinter yourself and try to please everyone, you can't.

—Annie Leibovitz

Today's priorities:

_____

_____

Tasks that will move me toward my goals: *Rank*

☐ _____ | ___

☐ _____ | ___

☐ _____ | ___

☐ _____ | ___

☐ _____ | ___

☐ _____ | ___

☐ _____ | ___

☐ _____ | ___

☐ _____ | ___

Today I will take care of myself by:

_____

_____

Today I spent my time on:

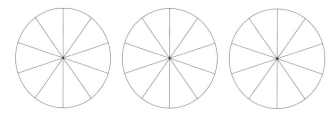

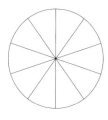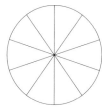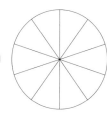

Today I am grateful for:

_____

_____

_____

_____

_____

_____

_____

Date: _____

I always believed that one woman's success can only help another woman's success.

—Gloria Vanderbilt

Today's priorities:

_____

_____

Tasks that will move me toward my goals: *Rank*

☐ _____ |____

☐ _____ |____

☐ _____ |____

☐ _____ |____

☐ _____ |____

☐ _____ |____

☐ _____ |____

☐ _____ |____

☐ _____ |____

Today I will take care of myself by:

_____

_____

56

Today I spent my time on:

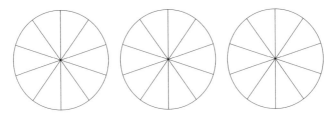

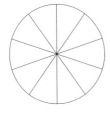 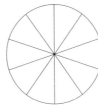 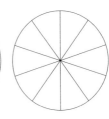

_____   _____   _____

_____   _____   _____

Today I am grateful for:

_____

_____

_____

_____

_____

_____

_____

Date: _____

If you can't go straight ahead, you go around the corner.

—**Cher**

Today's priorities:

_____

_____

Tasks that will move me toward my goals: *Rank*

☐ _____ | ____

☐ _____ | ____

☐ _____ | ____

☐ _____ | ____

☐ _____ | ____

☐ _____ | ____

☐ _____ | ____

☐ _____ | ____

☐ _____ | ____

Today I will take care of myself by:

_____

_____

Today I spent my time on:

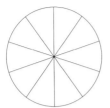 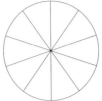 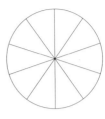

——————————— ——————————— ———————————

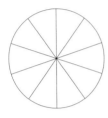 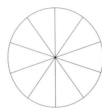 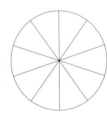

——————————— ——————————— ———————————

Today I am grateful for:

_____

_____

_____

_____

_____

_____

_____

Date: _____

Meditation and praying changes your spirit into something positive. If it is already positive, it makes it better.

—Tina Turner

Today's priorities:

_____

_____

Tasks that will move me toward my goals: *Rank*

☐ _____ |____

☐ _____ |____

☐ _____ |____

☐ _____ |____

☐ _____ |____

☐ _____ |____

☐ _____ |____

☐ _____ |____

☐ _____ |____

Today I will take care of myself by:

_____

_____

Today I spent my time on:

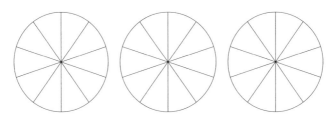

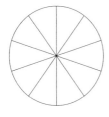
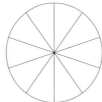
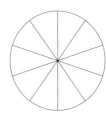

_____   _____   _____

_____   _____   _____

Today I am grateful for:

_____

_____

_____

_____

_____

_____

_____

Date: _____

Delete the negative; accentuate the positive.

—Donna Karan

Today's priorities:

_____

_____

Tasks that will move me toward my goals: *Rank*

☐ _____ |____

☐ _____ |____

☐ _____ |____

☐ _____ |____

☐ _____ |____

☐ _____ |____

☐ _____ |____

☐ _____ |____

☐ _____ |____

Today I will take care of myself by:

_____

_____

Today I spent my time on:

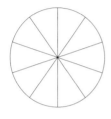
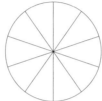
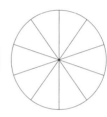

_____   _____   _____

_____   _____   _____

Today I am grateful for:

_____

_____

_____

_____

_____

_____

_____

Date: _____

Never get so busy making a living that you forget to make a life.
—Dolly Parton

Today's priorities:

_____

_____

Tasks that will move me toward my goals: **Rank**

☐ _____ |____

☐ _____ |____

☐ _____ |____

☐ _____ |____

☐ _____ |____

☐ _____ |____

☐ _____ |____

☐ _____ |____

☐ _____ |____

Today I will take care of myself by:

_____

_____

Today I spent my time on:

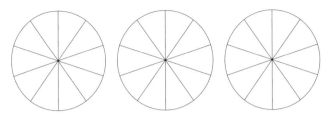

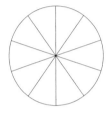
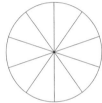
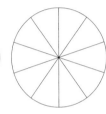

_____   _____   _____

Today I am grateful for:

_____

_____

_____

_____

_____

_____

_____

Date: _____

If you think taking care of yourself is selfish, change your mind. If you don't, you're simply ducking your responsibilities.

—Ann Richards

Today's priorities:

_____

_____

Tasks that will move me toward my goals: *Rank*

☐ _____ | ___

☐ _____ | ___

☐ _____ | ___

☐ _____ | ___

☐ _____ | ___

☐ _____ | ___

☐ _____ | ___

☐ _____ | ___

☐ _____ | ___

Today I will take care of myself by:

_____

_____

Today I spent my time on:

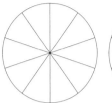 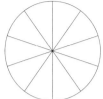 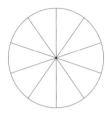

_____   _____   _____

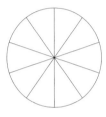 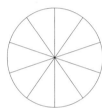 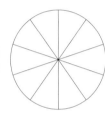

_____   _____   _____

Today I am grateful for:

_____

_____

_____

_____

_____

_____

_____

Date: _____

Burnout is about resentment. Preventing it is about knowing yourself well enough to know what it is you're giving up that makes you resentful.
—Marissa Mayer

Today's priorities:

_____

_____

Tasks that will move me toward my goals: *Rank*

☐ _____ |_____

☐ _____ |_____

☐ _____ |_____

☐ _____ |_____

☐ _____ |_____

☐ _____ |_____

☐ _____ |_____

☐ _____ |_____

☐ _____ |_____

Today I will take care of myself by:

_____

_____

Today I spent my time on:

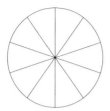 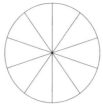 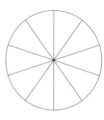

_____   _____   _____

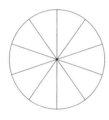 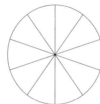 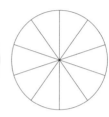

_____   _____   _____

Today I am grateful for:

_____

_____

_____

_____

_____

_____

_____

_____

Date: _____

Normal is not something to aspire to, it's something to get away from.
—Jodie Foster

Today's priorities:

_____

_____

Tasks that will move me toward my goals: *Rank*

☐ _____ | _____

☐ _____ | _____

☐ _____ | _____

☐ _____ | _____

☐ _____ | _____

☐ _____ | _____

☐ _____ | _____

☐ _____ | _____

☐ _____ | _____

Today I will take care of myself by:

_____

_____

Today I spent my time on:

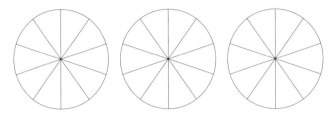

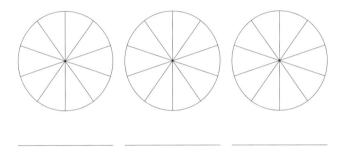

Today I am grateful for:

Date: _____

If you're someone people count on, particularly in difficult moments, that's a sign of a life lived honorably.

—Rachel Maddow

Today's priorities:

_____

_____

Tasks that will move me toward my goals: *Rank*

☐ _____ |____

☐ _____ |____

☐ _____ |____

☐ _____ |____

☐ _____ |____

☐ _____ |____

☐ _____ |____

☐ _____ |____

☐ _____ |____

Today I will take care of myself by:

_____

_____

Today I spent my time on:

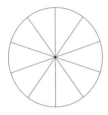 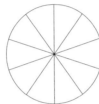 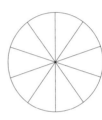

_____   _____   _____

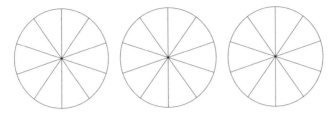

_____   _____   _____

Today I am grateful for:

_____

_____

_____

_____

_____

_____

_____

Date: _____

Done is better than perfect.

—Sheryl Sandberg

Today's priorities:

_____

_____

Tasks that will move me toward my goals: *Rank*

☐ _____ | _____

☐ _____ | _____

☐ _____ | _____

☐ _____ | _____

☐ _____ | _____

☐ _____ | _____

☐ _____ | _____

☐ _____ | _____

☐ _____ | _____

Today I will take care of myself by:

_____

_____

Today I spent my time on:

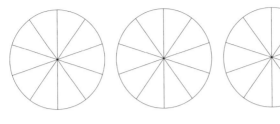

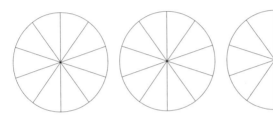

Today I am grateful for:

_____

_____

_____

_____

_____

_____

_____

Date: _____

The way to get started is to quit talking and begin doing.

—Walt Disney

Today's priorities:

_____

_____

Tasks that will move me toward my goals: *Rank*

☐ _____ | ___

☐ _____ | ___

☐ _____ | ___

☐ _____ | ___

☐ _____ | ___

☐ _____ | ___

☐ _____ | ___

☐ _____ | ___

☐ _____ | ___

Today I will take care of myself by:

_____

_____

Today I spent my time on:

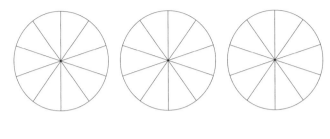

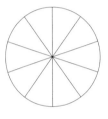
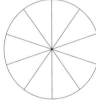
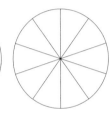

_____   _____   _____

_____   _____   _____

Today I am grateful for:

_____

_____

_____

_____

_____

_____

_____

Date: _____

You can't be that kid standing at the top of the waterslide, overthinking it. You have to go down the chute.

—Tina Fey

Today's priorities:

_____

_____

Tasks that will move me toward my goals: *Rank*

☐ _____ | ____

☐ _____ | ____

☐ _____ | ____

☐ _____ | ____

☐ _____ | ____

☐ _____ | ____

☐ _____ | ____

☐ _____ | ____

☐ _____ | ____

Today I will take care of myself by:

_____

_____

Today I spent my time on:

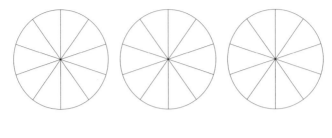

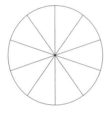 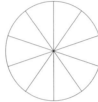 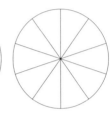

_____   _____   _____

Today I am grateful for:

_____

_____

_____

_____

_____

_____

_____

Date: _____

Whatever it is that you think you want to do, and whatever it is that you think stands between you and that, stop making excuses. You can do anything.

—Katia Beauchamp

Today's priorities:

_____

_____

Tasks that will move me toward my goals: *Rank*

☐ _____ |___

☐ _____ |___

☐ _____ |___

☐ _____ |___

☐ _____ |___

☐ _____ |___

☐ _____ |___

☐ _____ |___

☐ _____ |___

Today I will take care of myself by:

_____

_____

80

Today I spent my time on:

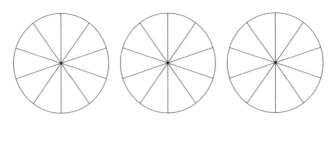

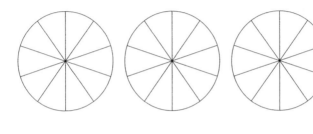

Today I am grateful for:

_____

_____

_____

_____

_____

_____

_____

Date: _____

It feels good. Kind of like when you have to shut your computer down, just sometimes when it goes crazy, you just shut it down and when you turn it on, it's okay again. That's what meditation is to me.

—Ellen DeGeneres

Today's priorities:

_____

_____

Tasks that will move me toward my goals: *Rank*

☐ _____ | ____

☐ _____ | ____

☐ _____ | ____

☐ _____ | ____

☐ _____ | ____

☐ _____ | ____

☐ _____ | ____

☐ _____ | ____

☐ _____ | ____

Today I will take care of myself by:

_____

_____

Today I spent my time on:

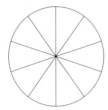 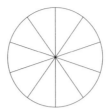 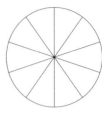

_____ _____ _____

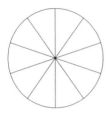  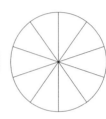

_____ _____ _____

Today I am grateful for:

_____

_____

_____

_____

_____

_____

_____

Date: _____

Above all, be the heroine of your life, not the victim.

—Nora Ephron

Today's priorities:

_____

_____

Tasks that will move me toward my goals: *Rank*

☐ _____ |____

☐ _____ |____

☐ _____ |____

☐ _____ |____

☐ _____ |____

☐ _____ |____

☐ _____ |____

☐ _____ |____

☐ _____ |____

Today I will take care of myself by:

_____

_____

Today I spent my time on:

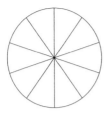 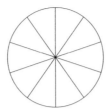 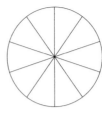

_____   _____   _____

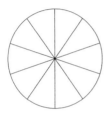 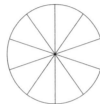 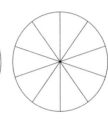

_____   _____   _____

Today I am grateful for:

_____

_____

_____

_____

_____

_____

_____

Date: _____

We think, mistakenly, that success is the result of the amount of time we put in at work, instead of the quality of time we put in.

—Arianna Huffington

Today's priorities:

_____

_____

Tasks that will move me toward my goals: *Rank*

☐ _____ | _____

☐ _____ | _____

☐ _____ | _____

☐ _____ | _____

☐ _____ | _____

☐ _____ | _____

☐ _____ | _____

☐ _____ | _____

☐ _____ | _____

Today I will take care of myself by:

_____

_____

Today I spent my time on:

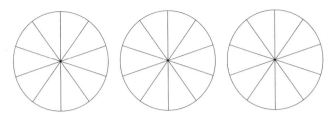

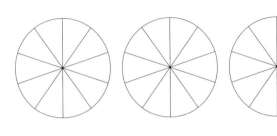

Today I am grateful for:

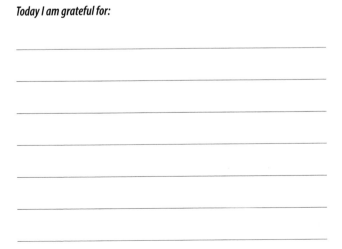

Look your best. Who said love is blind?

—Mae West

Today's priorities:

_____

_____

Tasks that will move me toward my goals: *Rank*

☐ _____ | _____

☐ _____ | _____

☐ _____ | _____

☐ _____ | _____

☐ _____ | _____

☐ _____ | _____

☐ _____ | _____

☐ _____ | _____

☐ _____ | _____

Today I will take care of myself by:

_____

_____

Today I spent my time on:

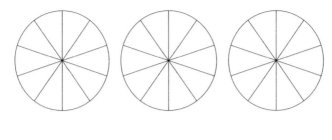

_____   _____   _____

_____   _____   _____

Today I am grateful for:

_____

_____

_____

_____

_____

_____

_____

Date: _____

When I'm hungry, I eat. When I'm thirsty, I drink. When I feel like saying something, I say it.

—Madonna

Today's priorities:

_____

_____

Tasks that will move me toward my goals: **Rank**

☐ _____ |

☐ _____ |

☐ _____ |

☐ _____ |

☐ _____ |

☐ _____ |

☐ _____ |

☐ _____ |

☐ _____ |

Today I will take care of myself by:

_____

_____

Today I spent my time on:

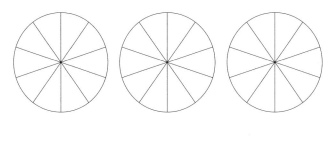

_____   _____   _____

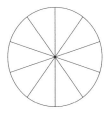 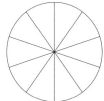 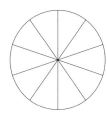

_____   _____   _____

Today I am grateful for:

_____

_____

_____

_____

_____

_____

_____

Date: _____

Power's not given to you. You have to take it.

—Beyoncé Knowles Carter

Today's priorities:

_____

_____

Tasks that will move me toward my goals: *Rank*

☐ _____ | _____

☐ _____ | _____

☐ _____ | _____

☐ _____ | _____

☐ _____ | _____

☐ _____ | _____

☐ _____ | _____

☐ _____ | _____

☐ _____ | _____

Today I will take care of myself by:

_____

_____

Today I spent my time on:

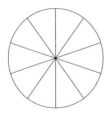 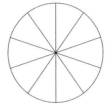 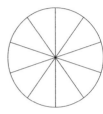

_____ _____ _____

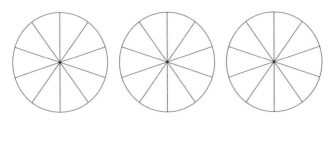

_____ _____ _____

Today I am grateful for:

_____

_____

_____

_____

_____

_____

_____

Date: _____

Doubt is a killer. You just have to know who you are and what you stand for.

—Jennifer Lopez

Today's priorities:

_____

_____

Tasks that will move me toward my goals: *Rank*

☐ _____ |

☐ _____ |

☐ _____ |

☐ _____ |

☐ _____ |

☐ _____ |

☐ _____ |

☐ _____ |

☐ _____ |

Today I will take care of myself by:

_____

_____

Today I spent my time on:

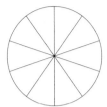 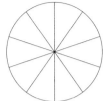 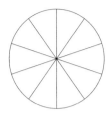

_____ _____ _____

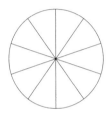 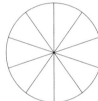 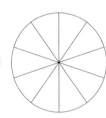

_____ _____ _____

Today I am grateful for:

_____

_____

_____

_____

_____

_____

_____

Date: _____

I really try to ask myself the question of nine. Will this matter in nine minutes, nine hours, nine days, nine weeks, nine months, or nine years? If it will truly matter for all of those, pay attention to it.

—Whitney Wolfe

Today's priorities:

_____

_____

Tasks that will move me toward my goals: *Rank*

☐ _____ | ____

☐ _____ | ____

☐ _____ | ____

☐ _____ | ____

☐ _____ | ____

☐ _____ | ____

☐ _____ | ____

☐ _____ | ____

☐ _____ | ____

Today I will take care of myself by:

_____

_____

Today I spent my time on:

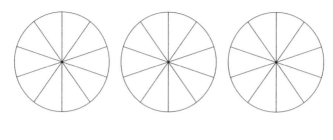

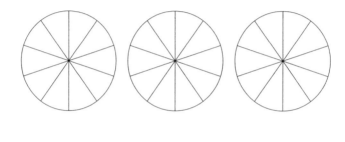

Today I am grateful for:

_____

_____

_____

_____

_____

_____

_____

Date: _____

We need to do a better job of putting ourselves higher on our own "to do" list.

—Michelle Obama

Today's priorities:

_____

_____

Tasks that will move me toward my goals: **Rank**

☐ _____ | ____

☐ _____ | ____

☐ _____ | ____

☐ _____ | ____

☐ _____ | ____

☐ _____ | ____

☐ _____ | ____

☐ _____ | ____

☐ _____ | ____

Today I will take care of myself by:

_____

_____

Today I spent my time on:

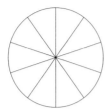 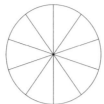 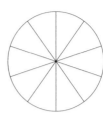

_____   _____   _____

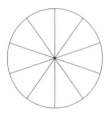 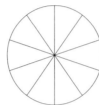 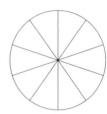

_____   _____   _____

Today I am grateful for:

_____

_____

_____

_____

_____

_____

_____

Date: _____

I'd rather regret the things I've done than regret the things I haven't done.

—Lucille Ball

Today's priorities:

_____

_____

Tasks that will move me toward my goals: *Rank*

☐ _____ | ____

☐ _____ | ____

☐ _____ | ____

☐ _____ | ____

☐ _____ | ____

☐ _____ | ____

☐ _____ | ____

☐ _____ | ____

☐ _____ | ____

Today I will take care of myself by:

_____

_____

Today I spent my time on:

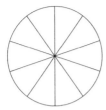 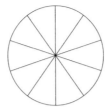 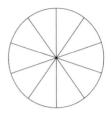

_____ _____ _____

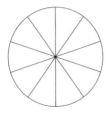 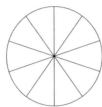 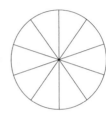

_____ _____ _____

Today I am grateful for:

_____

_____

_____

_____

_____

_____

_____

Date: _____

Don't confuse having a career with having a life.

—Hillary Clinton

Today's priorities:

_____

_____

Tasks that will move me toward my goals: *Rank*

☐ _____ |

☐ _____ |

☐ _____ |

☐ _____ |

☐ _____ |

☐ _____ |

☐ _____ |

☐ _____ |

☐ _____ |

Today I will take care of myself by:

_____

_____

Today I spent my time on:

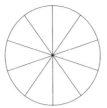 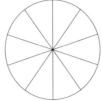 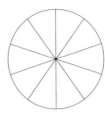

_____ _____ _____

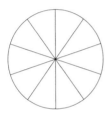 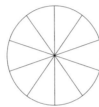 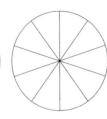

_____ _____ _____

Today I am grateful for:

_____

_____

_____

_____

_____

_____

_____

Date: _____

Protect the time and space in which you write. Keep everybody away from it, even the people who are most important to you.

—Zadie Smith

Today's priorities:

_____

_____

Tasks that will move me toward my goals: Rank

☐ _____ |____

☐ _____ |____

☐ _____ |____

☐ _____ |____

☐ _____ |____

☐ _____ |____

☐ _____ |____

☐ _____ |____

☐ _____ |____

Today I will take care of myself by:

_____

_____

Today I spent my time on:

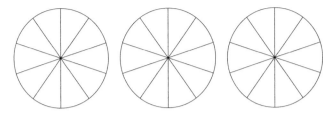

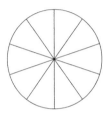 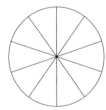 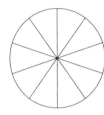

_____ _____ _____

Today I am grateful for:

_____

_____

_____

_____

_____

_____

_____

Date: _____

Life-fulfilling work is never about the money—when you feel true passion for something, you instinctively find ways to nurture it.

—Eileen Fisher

Today's priorities:

_____

_____

Tasks that will move me toward my goals: *Rank*

☐ _____ | _____

☐ _____ | _____

☐ _____ | _____

☐ _____ | _____

☐ _____ | _____

☐ _____ | _____

☐ _____ | _____

☐ _____ | _____

☐ _____ | _____

Today I will take care of myself by:

_____

_____

Today I spent my time on:

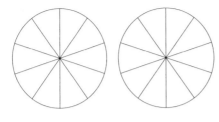 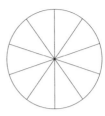

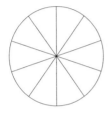 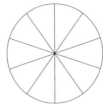 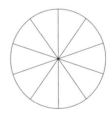

Today I am grateful for:

_____

_____

_____

_____

_____

_____

_____

Date: _____

The most courageous act is still to think for yourself. Aloud.

—Coco Chanel

Today's priorities:

_____

_____

Tasks that will move me toward my goals: *Rank*

☐ _____ | ____

☐ _____ | ____

☐ _____ | ____

☐ _____ | ____

☐ _____ | ____

☐ _____ | ____

☐ _____ | ____

☐ _____ | ____

☐ _____ | ____

Today I will take care of myself by:

_____

_____

Today I spent my time on:

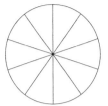 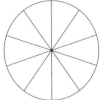 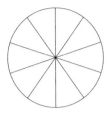

_____   _____   _____

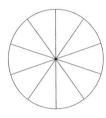 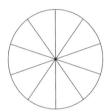 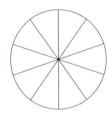

_____   _____   _____

Today I am grateful for:

_____

_____

_____

_____

_____

_____

_____

Date: _____

Step out of the history that is holding you back. Step into the new story you are willing to create.

—Oprah Winfrey

Today's priorities:

_____

_____

Tasks that will move me toward my goals: *Rank*

☐ _____ | _____

☐ _____ | _____

☐ _____ | _____

☐ _____ | _____

☐ _____ | _____

☐ _____ | _____

☐ _____ | _____

☐ _____ | _____

☐ _____ | _____

Today I will take care of myself by:

_____

_____

Today I spent my time on:

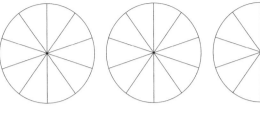
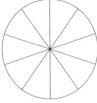

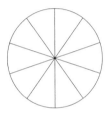
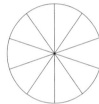
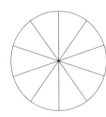

_____   _____   _____

_____   _____   _____

Today I am grateful for:

_____

_____

_____

_____

_____

_____

_____

Date: _____

You are the sky. Everything else is just the weather.

—Pema Chödrön

Today's priorities:

_____

_____

Tasks that will move me toward my goals:	*Rank*
☐ _____	|
☐ _____	|
☐ _____	|
☐ _____	|
☐ _____	|
☐ _____	|
☐ _____	|
☐ _____	|
☐ _____	|

Today I will take care of myself by:

_____

_____

Today I spent my time on:

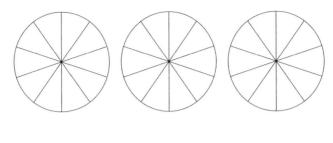

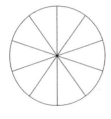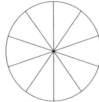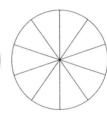

_____   _____   _____

_____   _____   _____

Today I am grateful for:

_____

_____

_____

_____

_____

_____

_____

Date: _____

Beware of monotony; it's the mother of all the deadly sins.

—Edith Wharton

Today's priorities:

_____

_____

Tasks that will move me toward my goals: *Rank*

☐ _____ | _____

☐ _____ | _____

☐ _____ | _____

☐ _____ | _____

☐ _____ | _____

☐ _____ | _____

☐ _____ | _____

☐ _____ | _____

☐ _____ | _____

Today I will take care of myself by:

_____

_____

Today I spent my time on:

 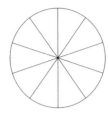 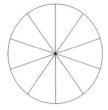

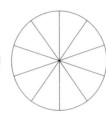 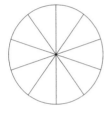

_____ _____ _____

Today I am grateful for:

_____

_____

_____

_____

_____

_____

_____

Date: _____

I build in fifteen-minute breaks so that I can take some quiet time and close on one meeting before I go to the next. I'm a big believer in taking time to pause and reflect, particularly when you're working on some of the big challenges in the world.

—Melinda Gates

Today's priorities:

_____

_____

Tasks that will move me toward my goals: *Rank*

☐ _____ |

☐ _____ |

☐ _____ |

☐ _____ |

☐ _____ |

☐ _____ |

☐ _____ |

☐ _____ |

Today I will take care of myself by:

_____

_____

Today I spent my time on:

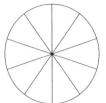  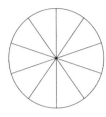

_____ _____ _____

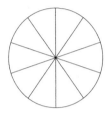 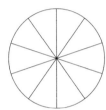 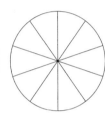

_____ _____ _____

Today I am grateful for:

_____

_____

_____

_____

_____

_____

_____

_____

Date: _____

If you're going through hell, keep going.

—Winston Churchill

Today's priorities:

_____

_____

Tasks that will move me toward my goals:　　　　　　　*Rank*

☐ _____ | ____

☐ _____ | ____

☐ _____ | ____

☐ _____ | ____

☐ _____ | ____

☐ _____ | ____

☐ _____ | ____

☐ _____ | ____

☐ _____ | ____

Today I will take care of myself by:

_____

_____

Today I spent my time on:

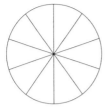 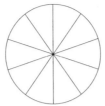 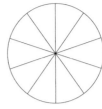

_____ _____ _____

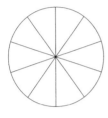 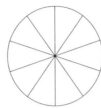 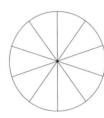

_____ _____ _____

Today I am grateful for:

_____

_____

_____

_____

_____

_____

_____

Date: _____

I enjoy life when things are happening. I don't care if it's good things or bad things. That means you're alive.

—Joan Rivers

Today's priorities:

_____

_____

Tasks that will move me toward my goals: *Rank*

☐ _____ | ____

☐ _____ | ____

☐ _____ | ____

☐ _____ | ____

☐ _____ | ____

☐ _____ | ____

☐ _____ | ____

☐ _____ | ____

☐ _____ | ____

Today I will take care of myself by:

_____

_____

Today I spent my time on:

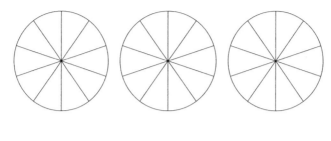

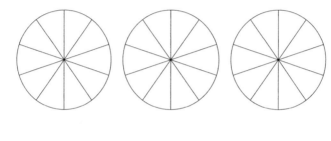

Today I am grateful for:

_____

_____

_____

_____

_____

_____

_____

Date: _____

It's never too late to make a comeback.

—Christina Katz

Today's priorities:

_____

_____

Tasks that will move me toward my goals: *Rank*

☐ _____ | _____

☐ _____ | _____

☐ _____ | _____

☐ _____ | _____

☐ _____ | _____

☐ _____ | _____

☐ _____ | _____

☐ _____ | _____

☐ _____ | _____

Today I will take care of myself by:

_____

_____

Today I spent my time on:

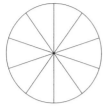 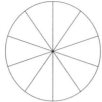 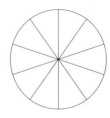

_____ _____ _____

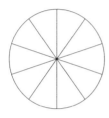 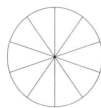 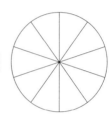

_____ _____ _____

Today I am grateful for:

_____

_____

_____

_____

_____

_____

_____

Date: _____

You can only really learn from failure . . . To win, you need to fail, and fail hard.

—Aisha Tyler

Today's priorities:

_____

_____

Tasks that will move me toward my goals: **Rank**

☐ _____ | ____

☐ _____ | ____

☐ _____ | ____

☐ _____ | ____

☐ _____ | ____

☐ _____ | ____

☐ _____ | ____

☐ _____ | ____

☐ _____ | ____

Today I will take care of myself by:

_____

_____

Today I spent my time on:

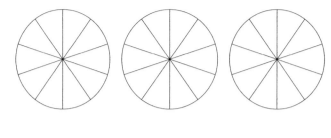

_____   _____   _____

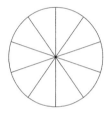 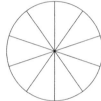 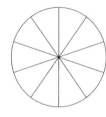

_____   _____   _____

Today I am grateful for:

_____

_____

_____

_____

_____

_____

_____

Date: _____

For fast-acting relief, try slowing down.

—Lily Tomlin

Today's priorities:

_____

_____

Tasks that will move me toward my goals: *Rank*

☐ _____ | ____

☐ _____ | ____

☐ _____ | ____

☐ _____ | ____

☐ _____ | ____

☐ _____ | ____

☐ _____ | ____

☐ _____ | ____

☐ _____ | ____

Today I will take care of myself by:

_____

_____

Today I spent my time on:

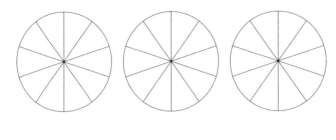

_____   _____   _____

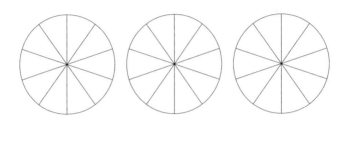

_____   _____   _____

Today I am grateful for:

_____

_____

_____

_____

_____

_____

Date: _____

It is our choices that show us who we truly are, far more than our abilities.

—Albus Dumbledore/J.K. Rowling

Today's priorities:

_____

_____

Tasks that will move me toward my goals: *Rank*

☐ _____ |____

☐ _____ |____

☐ _____ |____

☐ _____ |____

☐ _____ |____

☐ _____ |____

☐ _____ |____

☐ _____ |____

☐ _____ |____

Today I will take care of myself by:

_____

_____

Today I spent my time on:

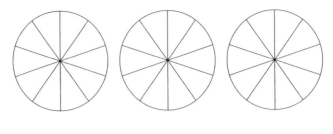

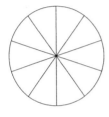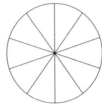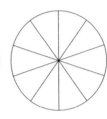

_____   _____   _____

Today I am grateful for:

_____

_____

_____

_____

_____

_____

_____

Date: _____

I've accepted my procrastination as part of who I am. As such, I do designate days where I allow time for procrastination.

—Issa Rae

Today's priorities:

_____

_____

Tasks that will move me toward my goals: *Rank*

☐ _____ | ____

☐ _____ | ____

☐ _____ | ____

☐ _____ | ____

☐ _____ | ____

☐ _____ | ____

☐ _____ | ____

☐ _____ | ____

☐ _____ | ____

Today I will take care of myself by:

_____

_____

Today I spent my time on:

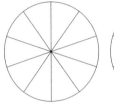

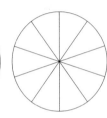

_____ _____ _____

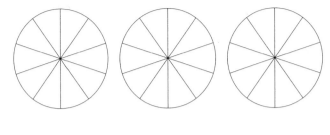

_____ _____ _____

Today I am grateful for:

_____

_____

_____

_____

_____

_____

_____

Date:_____

I still have highs and lows, maybe I don't cry salty tears as much.
—Sarah Silverman

Today's priorities:

_____

_____

Tasks that will move me toward my goals: *Rank*

☐ _____ | _____

☐ _____ | _____

☐ _____ | _____

☐ _____ | _____

☐ _____ | _____

☐ _____ | _____

☐ _____ | _____

☐ _____ | _____

☐ _____ | _____

Today I will take care of myself by:

_____

_____

Today I spent my time on:

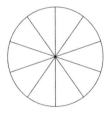 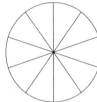 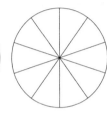

_____ _____ _____

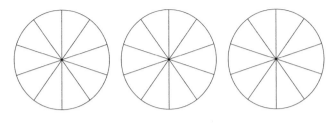

_____ _____ _____

Today I am grateful for:

_____

_____

_____

_____

_____

_____

_____

_____

Date: _____

To keep the body in good health is a duty . . . otherwise we shall not be able to keep our mind strong and clear.

—Buddha

Today's priorities:

_____

_____

Tasks that will move me toward my goals: *Rank*

☐ _____ |

☐ _____ |

☐ _____ |

☐ _____ |

☐ _____ |

☐ _____ |

☐ _____ |

☐ _____ |

☐ _____ |

Today I will take care of myself by:

_____

_____

Today I spent my time on:

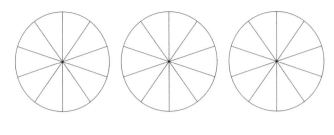

——————————— ——————————— ———————————

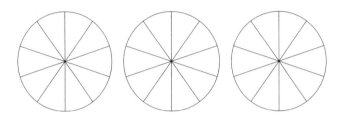

——————————— ——————————— ———————————

Today I am grateful for:

_____

_____

_____

_____

_____

_____

_____

Date: _____

Your body hears everything your mind says.

—Naomi Judd

Today's priorities:

_____

_____

Tasks that will move me toward my goals: *Rank*

☐ _____ | _____

☐ _____ | _____

☐ _____ | _____

☐ _____ | _____

☐ _____ | _____

☐ _____ | _____

☐ _____ | _____

☐ _____ | _____

☐ _____ | _____

Today I will take care of myself by:

_____

_____

Today I spent my time on:

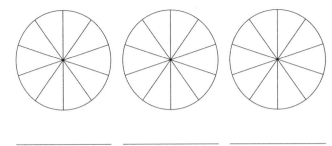

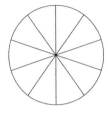
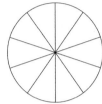
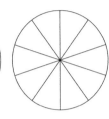

_____ _____ _____

_____ _____ _____

Today I am grateful for:

_____

_____

_____

_____

_____

_____

_____

Date: _____

I am so beautiful, sometimes people weep when they see me. And it has nothing to do with what I look like really, it is just that I gave myself the power to say that I am beautiful, and if I could do that, maybe there is hope for them, too. And the great divide between the beautiful and the ugly will cease to be. Because we are all what we choose.

—Margaret Cho

Today's priorities:

_____

_____

Tasks that will move me toward my goals: *Rank*

☐ _____ | ____

☐ _____ | ____

☐ _____ | ____

☐ _____ | ____

☐ _____ | ____

☐ _____ | ____

☐ _____ | ____

☐ _____ | ____

Today I will take care of myself by:

_____

_____

Today I spent my time on:

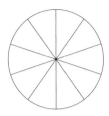 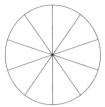 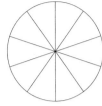

_____ _____ _____

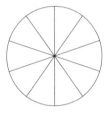 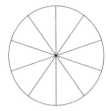 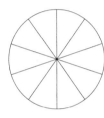

_____ _____ _____

Today I am grateful for:

_____

_____

_____

_____

_____

_____

_____

Date: _____

A mind set in its ways is wasted.

—Eric Schmidt

Today's priorities:

_____

_____

Tasks that will move me toward my goals: *Rank*

☐ _____ | ____

☐ _____ | ____

☐ _____ | ____

☐ _____ | ____

☐ _____ | ____

☐ _____ | ____

☐ _____ | ____

☐ _____ | ____

☐ _____ | ____

Today I will take care of myself by:

_____

_____

Today I spent my time on:

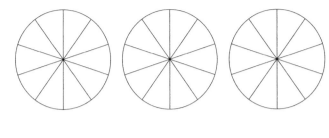

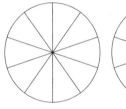 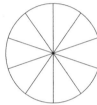 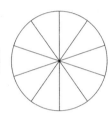

_____ _____ _____

_____ _____ _____

Today I am grateful for:

_____

_____

_____

_____

_____

_____

_____

Date: _____

Happiness comes from being who you actually are instead of who you think you are supposed to be.

—Shonda Rhimes

Today's priorities:

_____

_____

Tasks that will move me toward my goals:	Rank
☐ _____	|
☐ _____	|
☐ _____	|
☐ _____	|
☐ _____	|
☐ _____	|
☐ _____	|
☐ _____	|
☐ _____	|

Today I will take care of myself by:

_____

_____

Today I spent my time on:

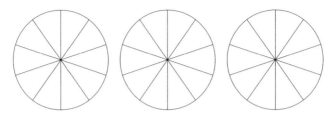

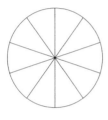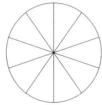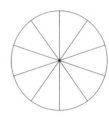

_____ _____ _____

Today I am grateful for:

_____

_____

_____

_____

_____

_____

_____

Date: _____

I have to realize that I'm not in control of everything, but I am in control of some things, and I am in control of my reactions. I am in control to my responses to pressure.

—Janelle Monae

Today's priorities:

_____

_____

Tasks that will move me toward my goals: *Rank*

☐ _____ | ____

☐ _____ | ____

☐ _____ | ____

☐ _____ | ____

☐ _____ | ____

☐ _____ | ____

☐ _____ | ____

☐ _____ | ____

☐ _____ | ____

Today I will take care of myself by:

_____

_____

Today I spent my time on:

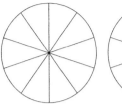 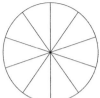 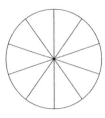

_____   _____   _____

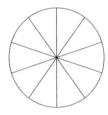 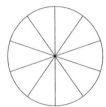 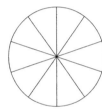

_____   _____   _____

Today I am grateful for:

_____

_____

_____

_____

_____

_____

_____

_____

Date: _____

It is health that is real wealth and not pieces of gold and silver.
—Mahatma Gandhi

Today's priorities:

_____

_____

Tasks that will move me toward my goals: *Rank*

☐ _____ | _____

☐ _____ | _____

☐ _____ | _____

☐ _____ | _____

☐ _____ | _____

☐ _____ | _____

☐ _____ | _____

☐ _____ | _____

☐ _____ | _____

Today I will take care of myself by:

_____

_____

Today I spent my time on:

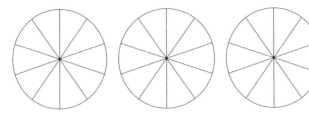

_____   _____   _____

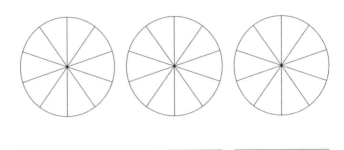

_____   _____   _____

Today I am grateful for:

_____

_____

_____

_____

_____

_____

_____

Date: _____

Surround yourself with a trusted and loyal team. It makes all the difference.

—Alison Pincus

Today's priorities:

_____

_____

Tasks that will move me toward my goals: *Rank*

☐ _____ | ____

☐ _____ | ____

☐ _____ | ____

☐ _____ | ____

☐ _____ | ____

☐ _____ | ____

☐ _____ | ____

☐ _____ | ____

☐ _____ | ____

Today I will take care of myself by:

_____

_____

Today I spent my time on:

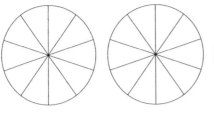 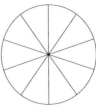

_____ _____ _____

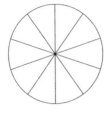 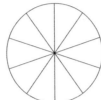 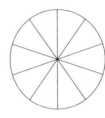

_____ _____ _____

Today I am grateful for:

_____

_____

_____

_____

_____

_____

_____

Date: _____

The difference between successful people and others is how long they spend time feeling sorry for themselves.

—Barbara Corcoran

Today's priorities:

_____

_____

Tasks that will move me toward my goals: *Rank*

☐ _____ | ____

☐ _____ | ____

☐ _____ | ____

☐ _____ | ____

☐ _____ | ____

☐ _____ | ____

☐ _____ | ____

☐ _____ | ____

☐ _____ | ____

Today I will take care of myself by:

_____

_____

Today I spent my time on:

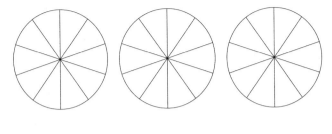

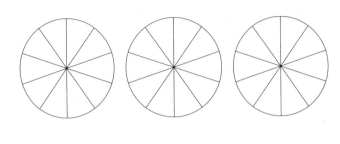

Today I am grateful for:

_____

_____

_____

_____

_____

_____

Date: _____

If you're creating anything at all, it's really dangerous to care about what people think.

—Kristen Wiig

Today's priorities:

_____

_____

Tasks that will move me toward my goals: **Rank**

☐ _____ | ____

☐ _____ | ____

☐ _____ | ____

☐ _____ | ____

☐ _____ | ____

☐ _____ | ____

☐ _____ | ____

☐ _____ | ____

☐ _____ | ____

Today I will take care of myself by:

_____

_____

Today I spent my time on:

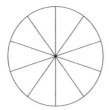 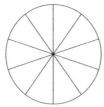 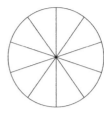

_____   _____   _____

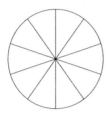 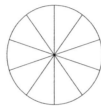 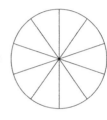

_____   _____   _____

Today I am grateful for:

_____

_____

_____

_____

_____

_____

_____

Date: _____

Worrying gets you nowhere. If you turn up worrying about how you're going to perform, you've already lost.

—Usain Bolt

Today's priorities:

_____

_____

Tasks that will move me toward my goals:　　　　　　　　**Rank**

☐ _____ |

☐ _____ |

☐ _____ |

☐ _____ |

☐ _____ |

☐ _____ |

☐ _____ |

☐ _____ |

☐ _____ |

Today I will take care of myself by:

_____

_____

Today I spent my time on:

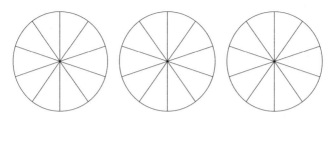

——————————— ——————————— ———————————

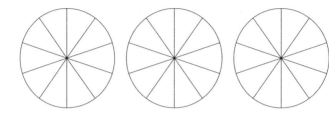

——————————— ——————————— ———————————

Today I am grateful for:

_____

_____

_____

_____

_____

_____

_____

Date: _____

Spread love everywhere you go. Let no one ever come to you without leaving happier.

—Mother Teresa

Today's priorities:

_____

_____

Tasks that will move me toward my goals: **Rank**

☐ _____ | ____

☐ _____ | ____

☐ _____ | ____

☐ _____ | ____

☐ _____ | ____

☐ _____ | ____

☐ _____ | ____

☐ _____ | ____

☐ _____ | ____

Today I will take care of myself by:

_____

_____

Today I spent my time on:

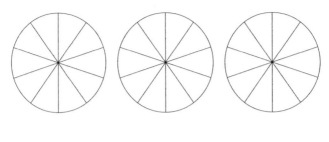

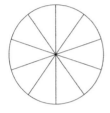 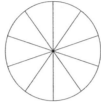 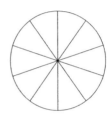

Today I am grateful for:

_____

_____

_____

_____

_____

_____

_____

Date: _____

Perfection is the death of all good things, perfection is the death of pleasure, it's the death of productivity, it's the death of efficiency, it's the death of joy.

—Elizabeth Gilbert

Today's priorities:

_____

_____

Tasks that will move me toward my goals: *Rank*

☐ _____ | _____

☐ _____ | _____

☐ _____ | _____

☐ _____ | _____

☐ _____ | _____

☐ _____ | _____

☐ _____ | _____

☐ _____ | _____

☐ _____ | _____

Today I will take care of myself by:

_____

_____

Today I spent my time on:

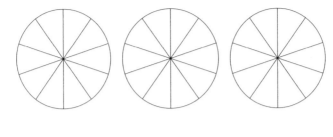

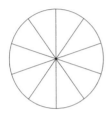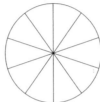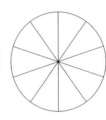

Today I am grateful for:

_____

_____

_____

_____

_____

_____

_____

Date: _____

Learn from the mistakes of others. You can't live long enough to make them all yourself.

—Eleanor Roosevelt

Today's priorities:

_____

_____

Tasks that will move me toward my goals: *Rank*

☐ _____ |____

☐ _____ |____

☐ _____ |____

☐ _____ |____

☐ _____ |____

☐ _____ |____

☐ _____ |____

☐ _____ |____

☐ _____ |____

Today I will take care of myself by:

_____

_____

Today I spent my time on:

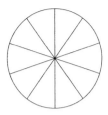
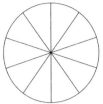
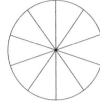

_____   _____   _____

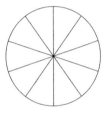
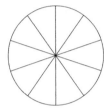
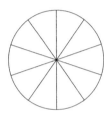

_____   _____   _____

Today I am grateful for:

_____

_____

_____

_____

_____

_____

_____

Date: _____

You can't be brave if you've only had wonderful things happen to you.
—Mary Tyler Moore

Today's priorities:

_____

_____

Tasks that will move me toward my goals: *Rank*

☐ _____ | ____

☐ _____ | ____

☐ _____ | ____

☐ _____ | ____

☐ _____ | ____

☐ _____ | ____

☐ _____ | ____

☐ _____ | ____

☐ _____ | ____

Today I will take care of myself by:

_____

_____

Today I spent my time on:

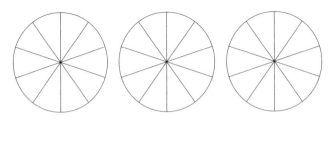

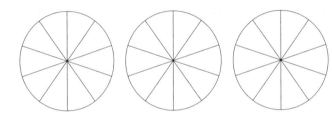

Today I am grateful for:

_____

_____

_____

_____

_____

_____

_____

Date: _____

Always remember that you are absolutely unique. Just like everyone else.
—Margaret Mead

Today's priorities:

_____

_____

Tasks that will move me toward my goals: *Rank*

☐ _____ |____

☐ _____ |____

☐ _____ |____

☐ _____ |____

☐ _____ |____

☐ _____ |____

☐ _____ |____

☐ _____ |____

☐ _____ |____

Today I will take care of myself by:

_____

_____

164

Today I spent my time on:

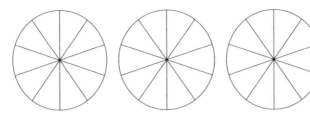

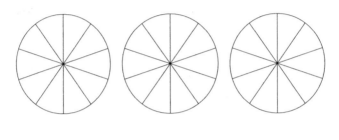

Today I am grateful for:

_____

_____

_____

_____

_____

_____

_____

Date: _____

Drama is very important in life: You have to come on with a bang. You never want to go out with a whimper.

—Julia Child

Today's priorities:

_____

_____

Tasks that will move me toward my goals: *Rank*

☐ _____ |____

☐ _____ |____

☐ _____ |____

☐ _____ |____

☐ _____ |____

☐ _____ |____

☐ _____ |____

☐ _____ |____

☐ _____ |____

Today I will take care of myself by:

_____

_____

Today I spent my time on:

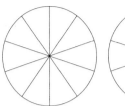 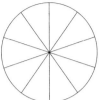 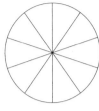

——————————— ——————————— ———————————

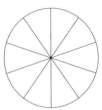 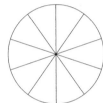 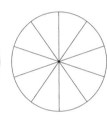

——————————— ——————————— ———————————

Today I am grateful for:

_____

_____

_____

_____

_____

_____

_____

Date: _____

A man who dares to waste one hour of time has not discovered the value of life.

—Charles Darwin

Today's priorities:

_____

_____

Tasks that will move me toward my goals: *Rank*

☐ _____ | ___

☐ _____ | ___

☐ _____ | ___

☐ _____ | ___

☐ _____ | ___

☐ _____ | ___

☐ _____ | ___

☐ _____ | ___

☐ _____ | ___

Today I will take care of myself by:

_____

_____

Today I spent my time on:

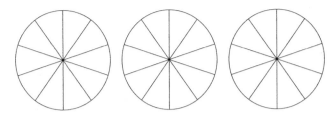

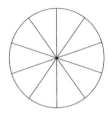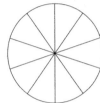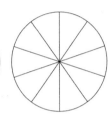

_____   _____   _____

_____   _____   _____

Today I am grateful for:

_____

_____

_____

_____

_____

_____

_____

_____

Date: _____

Nobody can go back and start a new beginning, but anyone can start today and make a new ending.

—Maria Robinson

Today's priorities:

_____

_____

Tasks that will move me toward my goals: *Rank*

☐ _____ | _____

☐ _____ | _____

☐ _____ | _____

☐ _____ | _____

☐ _____ | _____

☐ _____ | _____

☐ _____ | _____

☐ _____ | _____

☐ _____ | _____

Today I will take care of myself by:

_____

_____

Today I spent my time on:

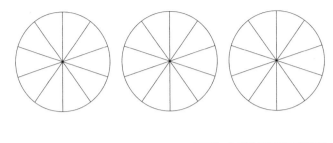

_____   _____   _____

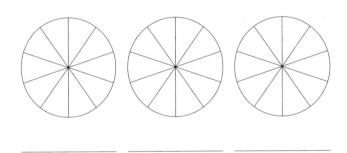

_____   _____   _____

Today I am grateful for:

_____

_____

_____

_____

_____

_____

_____

Date: _____

You can't do a good job if your job is all you do.

—Katie Thurmes

Today's priorities:

_____

_____

Tasks that will move me toward my goals: *Rank*

☐ _____ | ____

☐ _____ | ____

☐ _____ | ____

☐ _____ | ____

☐ _____ | ____

☐ _____ | ____

☐ _____ | ____

☐ _____ | ____

☐ _____ | ____

Today I will take care of myself by:

_____

_____

Today I spent my time on:

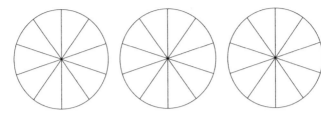

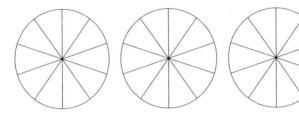

_____   _____   _____

Today I am grateful for:

_____

_____

_____

_____

_____

_____

_____

Date: _____

Smiling is definitely one of the best beauty remedies. If you have a good sense of humor and a good approach to life, that's beautiful.

—Rashida Jones

Today's priorities:

_____

_____

Tasks that will move me toward my goals: *Rank*

☐ _____ | ____

☐ _____ | ____

☐ _____ | ____

☐ _____ | ____

☐ _____ | ____

☐ _____ | ____

☐ _____ | ____

☐ _____ | ____

☐ _____ | ____

Today I will take care of myself by:

_____

_____

Today I spent my time on:

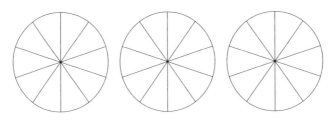

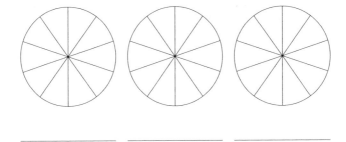

Today I am grateful for:

_____

_____

_____

_____

_____

_____

_____

_____

Date: _____

I think everybody should get rich and famous and do everything they ever dreamed of so they can see that it's not the answer.

—Jim Carrey

Today's priorities:

_____

_____

Tasks that will move me toward my goals: *Rank*

☐ _____ |____

☐ _____ |____

☐ _____ |____

☐ _____ |____

☐ _____ |____

☐ _____ |____

☐ _____ |____

☐ _____ |____

☐ _____ |____

Today I will take care of myself by:

_____

_____

Today I spent my time on:

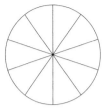 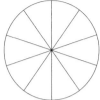 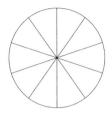

_____ _____ _____

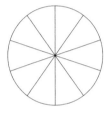 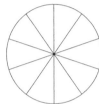 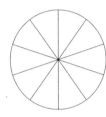

_____ _____ _____

Today I am grateful for:

_____

_____

_____

_____

_____

_____

_____

Date: _____

First of all, who cares if people hate you? There's always a guarantee that certain people will dislike you. There's never any guarantee that anyone will like you. So if anyone likes you at all, you've already won.
— **Chelsea Handler**

Today's priorities:

_____

_____

Tasks that will move me toward my goals: **Rank**

☐ _____ | ____

☐ _____ | ____

☐ _____ | ____

☐ _____ | ____

☐ _____ | ____

☐ _____ | ____

☐ _____ | ____

☐ _____ | ____

☐ _____ | ____

Today I will take care of myself by:

_____

_____

Today I spent my time on:

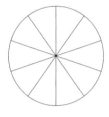 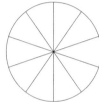 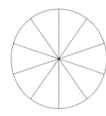

_____ _____ _____

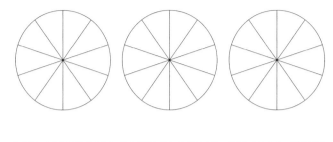

_____ _____ _____

Today I am grateful for:

_____

_____

_____

_____

_____

_____

_____

Date: _____

Be who you are and say what you feel, because those who mind don't matter and those who matter don't mind.

—Dr. Suess

Today's priorities:

_____

_____

Tasks that will move me toward my goals: *Rank*

☐ _____ |____

☐ _____ |____

☐ _____ |____

☐ _____ |____

☐ _____ |____

☐ _____ |____

☐ _____ |____

☐ _____ |____

☐ _____ |____

Today I will take care of myself by:

_____

_____

Today I spent my time on:

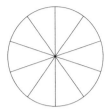 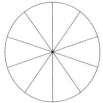 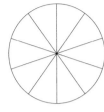

_____   _____   _____

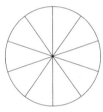 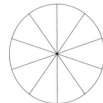 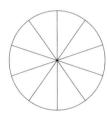

_____   _____   _____

Today I am grateful for:

_____

_____

_____

_____

_____

_____

_____

Date: _____

Use your health, even to the point of wearing it out. That is what it is for. Spend all you have before you die; do not outlive yourself.

—George Bernard Shaw

Today's priorities:

_____

_____

Tasks that will move me toward my goals: **Rank**

☐ _____ | ___

☐ _____ | ___

☐ _____ | ___

☐ _____ | ___

☐ _____ | ___

☐ _____ | ___

☐ _____ | ___

☐ _____ | ___

☐ _____ | ___

Today I will take care of myself by:

_____

_____

Today I spent my time on:

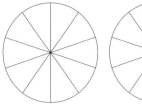  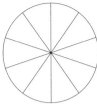

_____ _____ _____

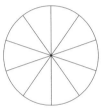 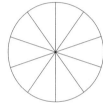 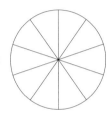

_____ _____ _____

Today I am grateful for:

_____

_____

_____

_____

_____

_____

_____

Date: _____

If you feel like there's something out there that you're supposed to be doing, if you have a passion for it, then stop wishing and just do it.
—Wanda Sykes

Today's priorities:

_____

_____

Tasks that will move me toward my goals: *Rank*

☐ _____ | ___

☐ _____ | ___

☐ _____ | ___

☐ _____ | ___

☐ _____ | ___

☐ _____ | ___

☐ _____ | ___

☐ _____ | ___

☐ _____ | ___

Today I will take care of myself by:

_____

_____

Today I spent my time on:

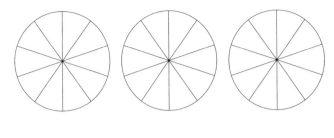

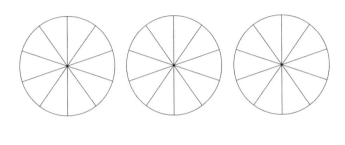

Today I am grateful for:

_____

_____

_____

_____

_____

_____

_____

Date: _____

Everyone is a complicated human being, and everyone is strong and weak and funny and scared.

—Laverne Cox

Today's priorities:

_____

_____

Tasks that will move me toward my goals: *Rank*

☐ _____ |____

☐ _____ |____

☐ _____ |____

☐ _____ |____

☐ _____ |____

☐ _____ |____

☐ _____ |____

☐ _____ |____

☐ _____ |____

Today I will take care of myself by:

_____

_____

Today I spent my time on:

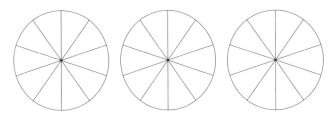

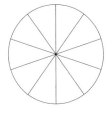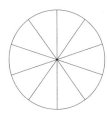

_____   _____   _____

_____   _____   _____

Today I am grateful for:

_____

_____

_____

_____

_____

_____

_____

Date: _____

My general attitude to life is to enjoy every minute of every day. I never do anything with a feeling of, "Oh God, I've got to do this today."

—Richard Branson

Today's priorities:

_____

_____

Tasks that will move me toward my goals: *Rank*

☐ _____ | ____

☐ _____ | ____

☐ _____ | ____

☐ _____ | ____

☐ _____ | ____

☐ _____ | ____

☐ _____ | ____

☐ _____ | ____

☐ _____ | ____

Today I will take care of myself by:

_____

_____

Today I spent my time on:

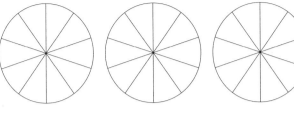

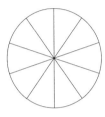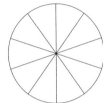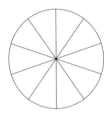

_____ _____ _____

Today I am grateful for:

_____

_____

_____

_____

_____

_____

_____

Date: _____

We are always getting ready to live but never living.
—Ralph Waldo Emerson

Today's priorities:

_____

_____

Tasks that will move me toward my goals: *Rank*

☐ _____ | ____

☐ _____ | ____

☐ _____ | ____

☐ _____ | ____

☐ _____ | ____

☐ _____ | ____

☐ _____ | ____

☐ _____ | ____

☐ _____ | ____

Today I will take care of myself by:

_____

_____

Today I spent my time on:

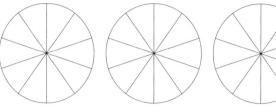

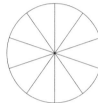

_____   _____   _____

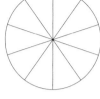

_____   _____   _____

Today I am grateful for:

_____

_____

_____

_____

_____

_____

_____

Date:_____

If your home environment is good and peaceful and easy, your life is better and easier.

—Lori Greiner

Today's priorities:

_____

_____

Tasks that will move me toward my goals: *Rank*

☐ _____ | ____

☐ _____ | ____

☐ _____ | ____

☐ _____ | ____

☐ _____ | ____

☐ _____ | ____

☐ _____ | ____

☐ _____ | ____

☐ _____ | ____

Today I will take care of myself by:

_____

_____

Today I spent my time on:

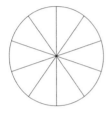 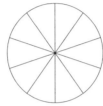 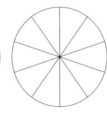

_____ _____ _____

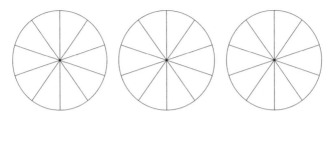

_____ _____ _____

Today I am grateful for:

_____

_____

_____

_____

_____

_____

_____

Date: _____

I don't know why femininity should be associated with weakness. Women should be free to express who they are without thinking, "I need to act like a man, or I need to tone it down to be successful." That's a very good way to keep women down.

—Zooey Deschanel

Today's priorities:

_____

_____

Tasks that will move me toward my goals:　　　　　　　*Rank*

☐ _____ |

☐ _____ |

☐ _____ |

☐ _____ |

☐ _____ |

☐ _____ |

☐ _____ |

☐ _____ |

Today I will take care of myself by:

_____

_____

Today I spent my time on:

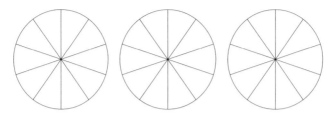

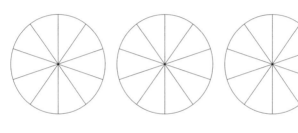

Today I am grateful for:

_____

_____

_____

_____

_____

_____

_____

Date: _____

To feel fulfillment and have a deeper level of understanding, personally, that is the most important thing.

—Alicia Keys

Today's priorities:

_____

_____

Tasks that will move me toward my goals: *Rank*

☐ _____ | ____

☐ _____ | ____

☐ _____ | ____

☐ _____ | ____

☐ _____ | ____

☐ _____ | ____

☐ _____ | ____

☐ _____ | ____

☐ _____ | ____

Today I will take care of myself by:

_____

_____

Today I spent my time on:

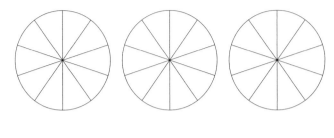

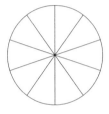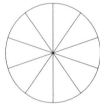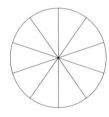

Today I am grateful for:

_____

_____

_____

_____

_____

_____

_____

Date: _____

To think in terms of either pessimism or optimism oversimplifies the truth. The problem is to see reality as it is.

—Thích Nhất Hạnh

Today's priorities:

_____

_____

Tasks that will move me toward my goals: **Rank**

☐ _____ | _____

☐ _____ | _____

☐ _____ | _____

☐ _____ | _____

☐ _____ | _____

☐ _____ | _____

☐ _____ | _____

☐ _____ | _____

☐ _____ | _____

Today I will take care of myself by:

_____

_____

Today I spent my time on:

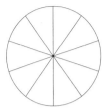 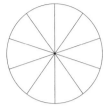 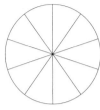

_____ _____ _____

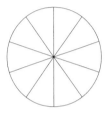 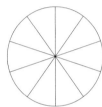 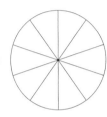

_____ _____ _____

Today I am grateful for:

_____

_____

_____

_____

_____

_____

_____

Date: _____

One friend with whom you have a lot in common is better than three with whom you struggle to find things to talk about.

—Mindy Kaling

Today's priorities:

_____

_____

Tasks that will move me toward my goals:	*Rank*
☐ _____	|
☐ _____	|
☐ _____	|
☐ _____	|
☐ _____	|
☐ _____	|
☐ _____	|
☐ _____	|
☐ _____	|

Today I will take care of myself by:

_____

_____

Today I spent my time on:

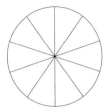

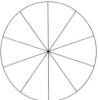

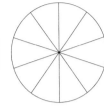

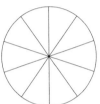

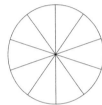

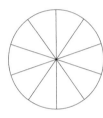

Today I am grateful for:

Date: _____

Run to the fire, don't hide from it.

—Meg Whitman

Today's priorities:

_____

_____

Tasks that will move me toward my goals: *Rank*

☐ _____ | ____

☐ _____ | ____

☐ _____ | ____

☐ _____ | ____

☐ _____ | ____

☐ _____ | ____

☐ _____ | ____

☐ _____ | ____

☐ _____ | ____

Today I will take care of myself by:

_____

_____

Today I spent my time on:

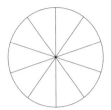 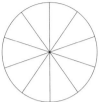 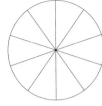

_____   _____   _____

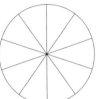 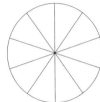 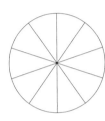

_____   _____   _____

Today I am grateful for:

_____

_____

_____

_____

_____

_____

_____

Date: _____

I have a simple philosophy: Fill what's empty. Empty what's full.
Scratch where it itches.

—Alice Roosevelt Longworth

Today's priorities:

_____

_____

Tasks that will move me toward my goals: *Rank*

☐ _____ | ___

☐ _____ | ___

☐ _____ | ___

☐ _____ | ___

☐ _____ | ___

☐ _____ | ___

☐ _____ | ___

☐ _____ | ___

☐ _____ | ___

Today I will take care of myself by:

_____

_____

Today I spent my time on:

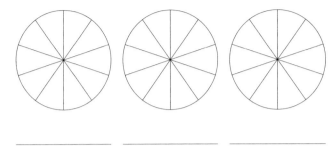

_____   _____   _____

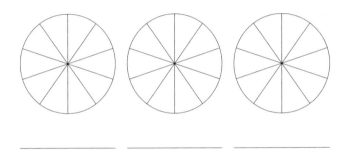

_____   _____   _____

Today I am grateful for:

_____

_____

_____

_____

_____

_____

_____

Date: _____

Happiness is the gradual realization of a worthy ideal or goal.
—Florence Nightingale

Today's priorities:

_____

_____

Tasks that will move me toward my goals: *Rank*

☐ _____ |___

☐ _____ |___

☐ _____ |___

☐ _____ |___

☐ _____ |___

☐ _____ |___

☐ _____ |___

☐ _____ |___

☐ _____ |___

Today I will take care of myself by:

_____

_____

Today I spent my time on:

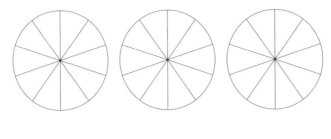

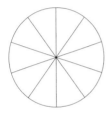
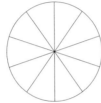
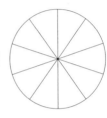

Today I am grateful for:

_____

_____

_____

_____

_____

_____

Date: _____

If you're walking down the right path and you're willing to keep walking, eventually you'll make progress.

—Barack Obama

Today's priorities:

_____

_____

Tasks that will move me toward my goals: *Rank*

☐ _____ | ____

☐ _____ | ____

☐ _____ | ____

☐ _____ | ____

☐ _____ | ____

☐ _____ | ____

☐ _____ | ____

☐ _____ | ____

☐ _____ | ____

Today I will take care of myself by:

_____

_____

Today I spent my time on:

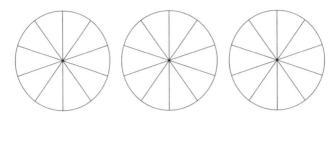

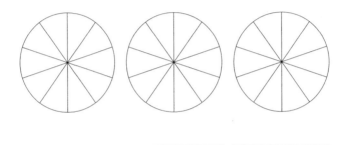

Today I am grateful for:

_____

_____

_____

_____

_____

_____

_____

Date: _____

We do not need magic to change the world, we carry all the power we need inside ourselves already: We have the power to imagine better.

—J.K. Rowling

Today's priorities:

_____

_____

Tasks that will move me toward my goals: *Rank*

☐ _____ | ____

☐ _____ | ____

☐ _____ | ____

☐ _____ | ____

☐ _____ | ____

☐ _____ | ____

☐ _____ | ____

☐ _____ | ____

☐ _____ | ____

Today I will take care of myself by:

_____

_____

Today I spent my time on:

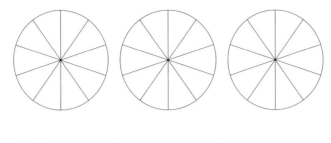

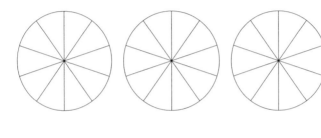

Today I am grateful for:

_____

_____

_____

_____

_____

_____

_____

Date: _____

I think I've discovered the secret of life—you just hang around until you get used to it.

—Charles Schulz

Today's priorities:

_____

_____

Tasks that will move me toward my goals: *Rank*

☐ _____ | ____

☐ _____ | ____

☐ _____ | ____

☐ _____ | ____

☐ _____ | ____

☐ _____ | ____

☐ _____ | ____

☐ _____ | ____

☐ _____ | ____

Today I will take care of myself by:

_____

_____

Today I spent my time on:

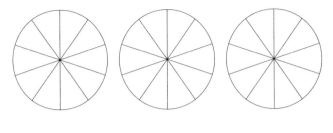

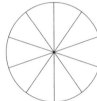

_____   _____   _____

_____   _____   _____

Today I am grateful for:

_____

_____

_____

_____

_____

_____

_____

Date: _____

I try to live in a little bit of my own joy and not let people steal it or take it.

—Hoda Kotb

Today's priorities:

_____

_____

Tasks that will move me toward my goals: **Rank**

☐ _____ | _____

☐ _____ | _____

☐ _____ | _____

☐ _____ | _____

☐ _____ | _____

☐ _____ | _____

☐ _____ | _____

☐ _____ | _____

☐ _____ | _____

Today I will take care of myself by:

_____

_____

Today I spent my time on:

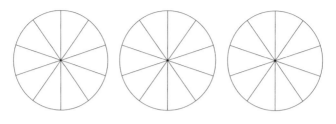

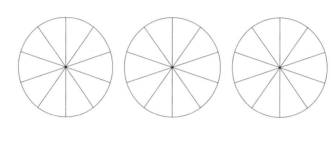

Today I am grateful for:

_____

_____

_____

_____

_____

_____

_____

Date: _____

When I'm tired, I rest. I say, "I can't be a superwoman today."
—**Jada Pinkett Smith**

Today's priorities:

_____

_____

Tasks that will move me toward my goals: *Rank*

☐ _____ | ___

☐ _____ | ___

☐ _____ | ___

☐ _____ | ___

☐ _____ | ___

☐ _____ | ___

☐ _____ | ___

☐ _____ | ___

☐ _____ | ___

Today I will take care of myself by:

_____

_____

Today I spent my time on:

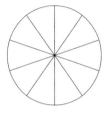 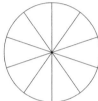 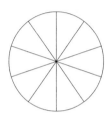

_____   _____   _____

_____   _____   _____

Today I am grateful for:

_____

_____

_____

_____

_____

_____

_____

Date: _____

Remembering you are going to die is the best way I know to avoid the trap of thinking you have something to lose. You are already naked. There's no reason not to follow your heart.

—Steve Jobs

Today's priorities:

_____

_____

Tasks that will move me toward my goals: **Rank**

☐ _____ | _____

☐ _____ | _____

☐ _____ | _____

☐ _____ | _____

☐ _____ | _____

☐ _____ | _____

☐ _____ | _____

☐ _____ | _____

☐ _____ | _____

Today I will take care of myself by:

_____

_____

Today I spent my time on:

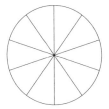 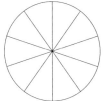 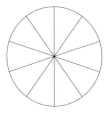

_____   _____   _____

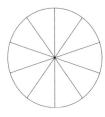 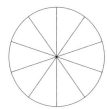 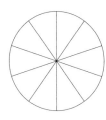

_____   _____   _____

Today I am grateful for:

_____

_____

_____

_____

_____

_____

_____

Date: _____

I firmly believe you never should spend your time being the former anything.

—Condoleezza Rice

Today's priorities:

_____

_____

Tasks that will move me toward my goals: **Rank**

☐ _____ | ____

☐ _____ | ____

☐ _____ | ____

☐ _____ | ____

☐ _____ | ____

☐ _____ | ____

☐ _____ | ____

☐ _____ | ____

☐ _____ | ____

Today I will take care of myself by:

_____

_____

Today I spent my time on:

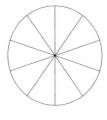 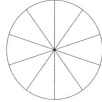 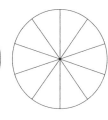

_____   _____   _____

_____   _____   _____

Today I am grateful for:

_____

_____

_____

_____

_____

_____

_____

Date: _____

The first step to getting the things you want out of life is this: Decide what you want.

—Ben Stein

Today's priorities:

_____

_____

Tasks that will move me toward my goals:	Rank
☐ _____	| ____
☐ _____	| ____
☐ _____	| ____
☐ _____	| ____
☐ _____	| ____
☐ _____	| ____
☐ _____	| ____
☐ _____	| ____
☐ _____	| ____

Today I will take care of myself by:

_____

_____

Today I spent my time on:

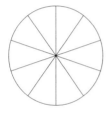 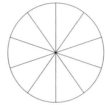 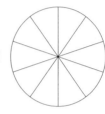

_____   _____   _____

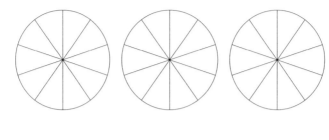

_____   _____   _____

Today I am grateful for:

_____

_____

_____

_____

_____

_____

_____

Date: _____

Life is like riding a bicycle. To keep your balance you must keep moving!
—Albert Einstein

Today's priorities:

_____

_____

Tasks that will move me toward my goals: *Rank*

☐ _____ | ____

☐ _____ | ____

☐ _____ | ____

☐ _____ | ____

☐ _____ | ____

☐ _____ | ____

☐ _____ | ____

☐ _____ | ____

☐ _____ | ____

Today I will take care of myself by:

_____

_____

Today I spent my time on:

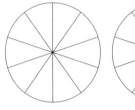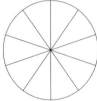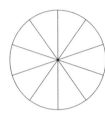

_____   _____   _____

_____   _____   _____

Today I am grateful for:

_____

_____

_____

_____

_____

_____

_____

Date: _____

Be easy on yourself. Have fun. Only hang around people that are positive and make you feel good. Anybody who doesn't make you feel good, kick them to the curb. And the earlier you start in your life the better.

—Amy Poehler

Today's priorities:

_____

_____

Tasks that will move me toward my goals: *Rank*

☐ _____ | ____

☐ _____ | ____

☐ _____ | ____

☐ _____ | ____

☐ _____ | ____

☐ _____ | ____

☐ _____ | ____

☐ _____ | ____

☐ _____ | ____

Today I will take care of myself by:

_____

_____

Today I spent my time on:

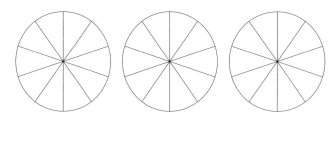

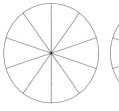

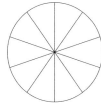

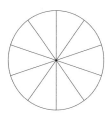

_____   _____   _____

_____   _____   _____

Today I am grateful for:

_____

_____

_____

_____

_____

_____

_____

THE SUPER WOMAN JOURNAL ✹ PLAN

In three words I can sum up everything I've learned about life: It goes on.

—Robert Frost

Today's priorities:

_____

_____

Tasks that will move me toward my goals: *Rank*

☐ _____ | ____

☐ _____ | ____

☐ _____ | ____

☐ _____ | ____

☐ _____ | ____

☐ _____ | ____

☐ _____ | ____

☐ _____ | ____

☐ _____ | ____

Today I will take care of myself by:

_____

_____

Today I spent my time on:

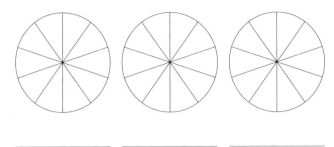

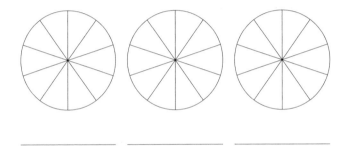

Today I am grateful for:

_____

_____

_____

_____

_____

_____

_____

Date: _____

People respond well to those that are sure of what they want.

—Anna Wintour

Today's priorities:

_____

_____

Tasks that will move me toward my goals: *Rank*

☐ _____ | _____

☐ _____ | _____

☐ _____ | _____

☐ _____ | _____

☐ _____ | _____

☐ _____ | _____

☐ _____ | _____

☐ _____ | _____

☐ _____ | _____

Today I will take care of myself by:

_____

_____

Today I spent my time on:

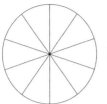 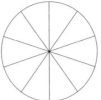 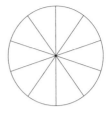

_____   _____   _____

 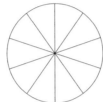 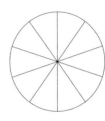

_____   _____   _____

Today I am grateful for:

_____

_____

_____

_____

_____

_____

_____

Date: _____

The secret of getting ahead is getting started.

—Mark Twain

Today's priorities:

_____

_____

Tasks that will move me toward my goals: *Rank*

☐ _____ | ____

☐ _____ | ____

☐ _____ | ____

☐ _____ | ____

☐ _____ | ____

☐ _____ | ____

☐ _____ | ____

☐ _____ | ____

☐ _____ | ____

Today I will take care of myself by:

_____

_____

Today I spent my time on:

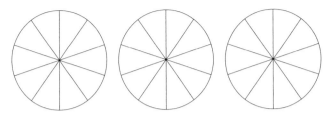

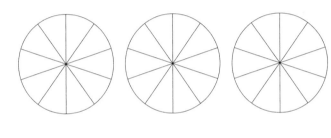

Today I am grateful for:

Date: _____

*Without leaps of imagination, or dreaming, we lose the excitement of
possibilities. Dreaming, after all, is a form of planning.*

—Glora Steinem

Today's priorities:

_____

_____

Tasks that will move me toward my goals: **Rank**

☐ _____ |

☐ _____ |

☐ _____ |

☐ _____ |

☐ _____ |

☐ _____ |

☐ _____ |

☐ _____ |

☐ _____ |

Today I will take care of myself by:

_____

_____

Today I spent my time on:

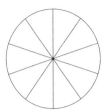 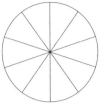 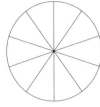

_____ _____ _____

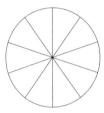 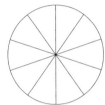 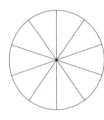

_____ _____ _____

Today I am grateful for:

_____

_____

_____

_____

_____

_____

_____

Date: _____

Don't count the days. Make the days count.

—Muhammad Ali

Today's priorities:

_____

_____

Tasks that will move me toward my goals: *Rank*

☐ _____ | ____

☐ _____ | ____

☐ _____ | ____

☐ _____ | ____

☐ _____ | ____

☐ _____ | ____

☐ _____ | ____

☐ _____ | ____

☐ _____ | ____

Today I will take care of myself by:

_____

_____

Today I spent my time on:

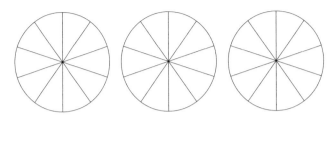

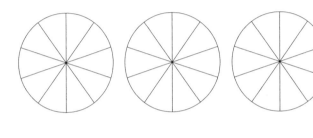

Today I am grateful for:

_____

_____

_____

_____

_____

_____

_____

Date: _____

You've gotta keep control of your time, and you can't unless you say no. You can't let people set your agenda in life.

—Warren Buffett

Today's priorities:

_____

_____

Tasks that will move me toward my goals: **Rank**

☐ _____ | _____

☐ _____ | _____

☐ _____ | _____

☐ _____ | _____

☐ _____ | _____

☐ _____ | _____

☐ _____ | _____

☐ _____ | _____

☐ _____ | _____

Today I will take care of myself by:

_____

_____

Today I spent my time on:

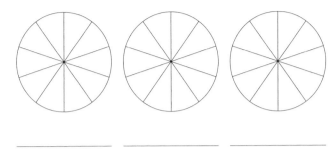

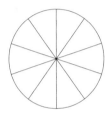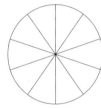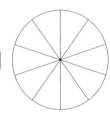

_____   _____   _____

_____   _____   _____

Today I am grateful for:

_____

_____

_____

_____

_____

_____

_____

Date: _____

I am not afraid . . . I was born to do this.

—Joan of Arc

Today's priorities:

_____

_____

Tasks that will move me toward my goals: *Rank*

☐ _____ | ____

☐ _____ | ____

☐ _____ | ____

☐ _____ | ____

☐ _____ | ____

☐ _____ | ____

☐ _____ | ____

☐ _____ | ____

☐ _____ | ____

Today I will take care of myself by:

_____

_____

Today I spent my time on:

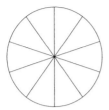 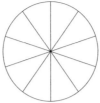 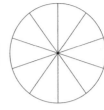

_____ _____ _____

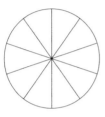 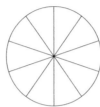 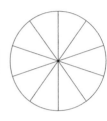

_____ _____ _____

Today I am grateful for:

_____

_____

_____

_____

_____

_____

_____

_____

Date: _____

When you're through changing, you're through.

—Martha Stewart

Today's priorities:

_____

_____

Tasks that will move me toward my goals: *Rank*

☐ _____ | _____

☐ _____ | _____

☐ _____ | _____

☐ _____ | _____

☐ _____ | _____

☐ _____ | _____

☐ _____ | _____

☐ _____ | _____

☐ _____ | _____

Today I will take care of myself by:

_____

_____

Today I spent my time on:

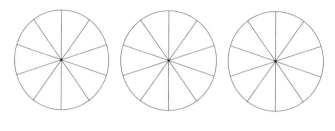

_____   _____   _____

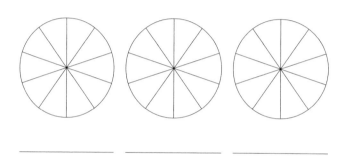

_____   _____   _____

Today I am grateful for:

_____

_____

_____

_____

_____

_____

_____

Date: _____

Wherever you go, there you are.

—Jon Kabat-Zinn

Today's priorities:

_____

_____

Tasks that will move me toward my goals: **Rank**

☐ _____ | ____

☐ _____ | ____

☐ _____ | ____

☐ _____ | ____

☐ _____ | ____

☐ _____ | ____

☐ _____ | ____

☐ _____ | ____

☐ _____ | ____

Today I will take care of myself by:

_____

_____

Today I spent my time on:

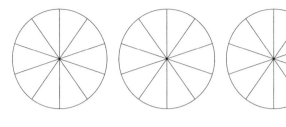

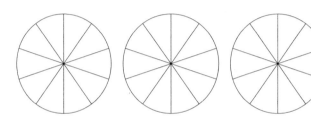

_____ _____ _____

Today I am grateful for:

_____

_____

_____

_____

_____

_____

_____

Date: _____

Noble deeds and hot baths are the best cures for depression.

—Dodie Smith

Today's priorities:

_____

_____

Tasks that will move me toward my goals: *Rank*

☐ _____ | ____

☐ _____ | ____

☐ _____ | ____

☐ _____ | ____

☐ _____ | ____

☐ _____ | ____

☐ _____ | ____

☐ _____ | ____

☐ _____ | ____

Today I will take care of myself by:

_____

_____

Today I spent my time on:

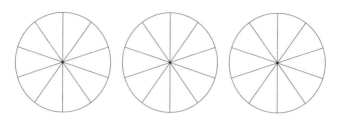

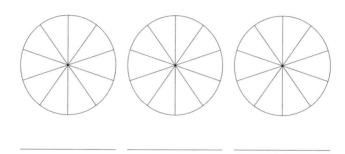

Today I am grateful for:

_____

_____

_____

_____

_____

_____

_____

Date: _____

Our life comes in segments, and we have to understand that we can have it all if we're not trying to do it all at once.

—Madeline Albright

Today's priorities:

_____

_____

Tasks that will move me toward my goals: *Rank*

☐ _____ |

☐ _____ |

☐ _____ |

☐ _____ |

☐ _____ |

☐ _____ |

☐ _____ |

☐ _____ |

☐ _____ |

Today I will take care of myself by:

_____

_____

Today I spent my time on:

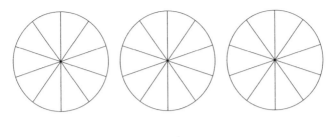

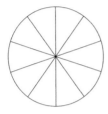 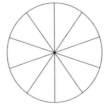 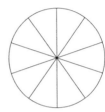

Today I am grateful for:

_____

_____

_____

_____

_____

_____

_____

Date: _____

Sitting with myself to find my truth wasn't easy but it wasn't the hardest part. The hardest part is living in accordance with it.

—Lavinia Errico

Today's priorities:

_____

_____

Tasks that will move me toward my goals: *Rank*

☐ _____ | ___

☐ _____ | ___

☐ _____ | ___

☐ _____ | ___

☐ _____ | ___

☐ _____ | ___

☐ _____ | ___

☐ _____ | ___

☐ _____ | ___

Today I will take care of myself by:

_____

_____

Today I spent my time on:

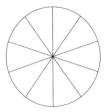 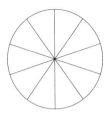

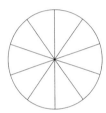 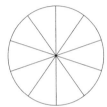 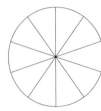

Today I am grateful for:

_____

_____

_____

_____

_____

_____

_____

Date: _____

The wound is the place where light enters you.

—Rumi

Today's priorities:

_____

_____

Tasks that will move me toward my goals: *Rank*

☐ _____ | ____

☐ _____ | ____

☐ _____ | ____

☐ _____ | ____

☐ _____ | ____

☐ _____ | ____

☐ _____ | ____

☐ _____ | ____

☐ _____ | ____

Today I will take care of myself by:

_____

_____

Today I spent my time on:

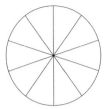 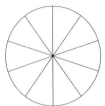 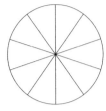

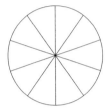 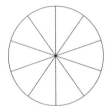 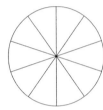

Today I am grateful for:

Date: _____

It is not because things are difficult that we do not dare, but because we do not dare, things are difficult.

—Seneca

Today's priorities:

_____

_____

Tasks that will move me toward my goals: **Rank**

☐ _____ | ____

☐ _____ | ____

☐ _____ | ____

☐ _____ | ____

☐ _____ | ____

☐ _____ | ____

☐ _____ | ____

☐ _____ | ____

☐ _____ | ____

Today I will take care of myself by:

_____

_____

Today I spent my time on:

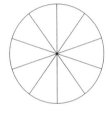 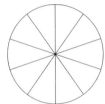 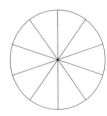

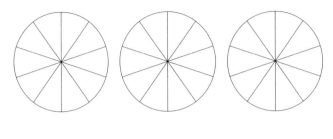

_____ _____ _____

_____ _____ _____

Today I am grateful for:

_____

_____

_____

_____

_____

_____

_____

Date: _____

*Authenticity is a collection of choices that we have to make every day.
It's about the choice to show up and be real. The choice to be honest.
The choice to let our true selves be seen.*

—Brené Brown

Today's priorities:

_____

_____

Tasks that will move me toward my goals: *Rank*

☐ _____ | ____

☐ _____ | ____

☐ _____ | ____

☐ _____ | ____

☐ _____ | ____

☐ _____ | ____

☐ _____ | ____

☐ _____ | ____

☐ _____ | ____

Today I will take care of myself by:

_____

_____

Today I spent my time on:

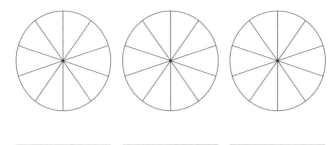

_____   _____   _____

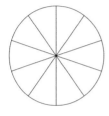
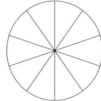
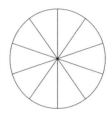

_____   _____   _____

Today I am grateful for:

_____

_____

_____

_____

_____

_____

_____

REWRITES

P eople change, goals change, priorities change. On the next pages, you'll find space to revisit your goals and priorities as needed. Just like any first draft, the goals and priorities you identified at the beginning of this journal will go through rewrites. Honor every chapter you write and edit. Don't rip any out, even though sometimes it feels like you want to. Your full story, with all of the plot twists and turns, is yours. Own it.

MY FINANCE GOALS

First Draft

Year 1: _____

_____

Year 3: _____

_____

Year 5: _____

_____

Year 7: _____

_____

Year 10: _____

_____

Rewrite #1

Year 1: _____

_____

Year 3: _____

_____

Year 5: _____

_____

Year 7: _____

_____

Year 10: _____

_____

Rewrite #2

Year 1: _____

_____

Year 3: _____

_____

Year 5: _____

_____

Year 7: _____

_____

Year 10: _____

_____

MY FAMILY GOALS

First Draft

Year 1: _____

_____

Year 3: _____

_____

Year 5: _____

_____

Year 7: _____

_____

Year 10: _____

_____

Rewrite #1

Year 1: _____

_____

Year 3: _____

_____

Year 5: _____

_____

Year 7: _____

_____

Year 10: _____

_____

Rewrite #2

Year 1: _____

_____

Year 3: _____

_____

Year 5: _____

_____

Year 7: _____

_____

Year 10: _____

_____

MY FUN GOALS

First Draft

Year 1: _____

_____

Year 3: _____

_____

Year 5: _____

_____

Year 7: _____

_____

Year 10: _____

_____

Rewrite #1

Year 1: _____

_____

Year 3: _____

_____

Year 5: _____

_____

Year 7: _____

_____

Year 10: _____

_____

Rewrite #2

Year 1: _____

_____

Year 3: _____

_____

Year 5: _____

_____

Year 7: _____

_____

Year 10: _____

_____

MY FITNESS GOALS

First Draft

Year 1: _____

_____

Year 3: _____

_____

Year 5: _____

_____

Year 7: _____

_____

Year 10: _____

_____

Rewrite #1

Year 1: _____

_____

Year 3: _____

_____

Year 5: _____

_____

Year 7: _____

_____

Year 10: _____

_____

Rewrite #2

Year 1: _____

_____

Year 3: _____

_____

Year 5: _____

_____

Year 7: _____

_____

Year 10: _____

_____

MY PRIORITIES

First Draft

1. Career: _____
2. Romance: _____
3. Family & Friends: _____
4. Physical Health: _____
5. Emotional Wellness: _____

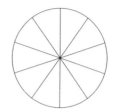

Total: 10 points

Rewrite #1

1. Career: _____
2. Romance: _____
3. Family & Friends: _____
4. Physical Health: _____
5. Emotional Wellness: _____

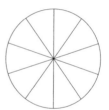

Total: 10 points

Rewrite #2

1. Career: _____
2. Romance: _____
3. Family & Friends: _____
4. Physical Health: _____
5. Emotional Wellness: _____

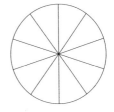

Total: 10 points

A purpose without a plan
is just a prayer.

MUSINGS